BUNCO KELLY AND OTHER

YARNS

OF PORTLAND AND NORTHWEST OREGON

BUNCO KELLY AND OTHER

YARNS

OF PORTLAND AND NORTHWEST OREGON

BY THOMAS K. WORCESTER   DRAWINGS BY ROBERT REYNOLDS

Based on the popular radio
series "Stories of Pacific Powerland"
narrated by Nelson Olmsted

TMS BOOK SERVICE
P.O. Box 1504
Beaverton, Oregon 97075

I.S.B.N. 0-911518-66-5

CONTENTS

INTRODUCTION

If "regurgitate" was a more acceptable word, it could be used in connection with this book and the stories in it. But, why not use it? If, as Webster says, regurgitate means "to become thrown or poured back," then it seems to fit, at least in my warped usage. For these yarns all have been told before, and now are collected from the pool of public literacy and poured back for another generation of readers.

The stories are historical, and generally true, as were those in the companion volume, THE STATE OF JEFFERSON AND OTHER YARNS. Basic facts have not been altered, but the writer has taken some liberties with dialogue attributed to various persons, though sometimes merely making a verbal quote from a written statement. Some of the stories are sad, others outright humorous, some are whimsical. All reflect, in a way, the human condition as Oregon was struggling through its larval stage.

As with the previous YARNS book, the stories are not the kind to cause disruptions in metagalaxies. Yet they reveal a spirit that was dominant in this young land: the spirit of discovery and development — of doing, if you will. And, they are character studies in the best sense.

But the stories are more than that, at least to the writer. They are a tribute to the man for whom I had the privilege of preparing them for oral presentation: Nelson Olmsted, for 16 years the narrator of Pacific Power & Light's "Stories of Pacific Powerland." Nelson is the consummate storyteller: intelligent, witty, reflective, folksy and multi-talented. Working with him during the eight years I wrote the 640-some radio scripts he narrated was one of the delights of my professional career. With his changes of voice and the characterizations he developed, Nelson could make a story come alive. And, he always seemed to know when a story had the quality that brought it above the ordinary.

Therefore, part of the challenge of retelling these stories in the written form was to see if they could maintain the same interest in the single plane of text that they did when spoken. I have tried to keep a similar "verbal" quality, which is easy for me because I "hear" the stories as I write them. I can only hope that readers, particularly younger readers, can, too.

Once again, the visual treatment by Robert Reynolds in this historical Whitman's Sampler enhances the volume, as did his imaginative interpretations in the previous YARNS book. These are not mere illustrations to support the text. They are cognitive art.

I would be remiss not to give general recognition to other writers and researchers who have helped keep good yarns such as these alive, particularly those persons involved in the Oregon Writers' Project, part of the Work Project Administration's Federal Writers' Project during the late 1930's. This program provided badly needed income for writers during the post-Depression recovery years, and through it developed a valuable resource of historical reference material that has been most useful to those of us who followed.

Clackamas, Oregon
January, 1983

TKW

Dedicated to a noted Frank.....

BUNCO KELLY

One day back in the 1890's, a British sea captain searched the Portland waterfront for an able-bodied seaman to make the long voyage from Portland to Australia with a load of lumber. Finally, in desperation, he approached a sleazy boardinghouse keeper known as Bunco Kelly:

"Kelly? Ah, good afternoon. I'm Captain Porter, of the *Warwick*. I'm told you might be able to help me."

"What is it you need, Captain?" Kelly responded.

"I sail at first light, and I'm one man short in my crew. I need a good seaman. I thought you might be able to use your 'persuasion' to find the right man for me."

Bunco Kelly knew what kind of persuasion Captain Porter meant, for in addition to running a rooming house for sailors, he was said to be able to fill a ship's crew on short notice. When it came to shanghaiing, Kelly had few peers. But, Bunco liked to play games, and he assumed an innocent air with the British captain. The little Irisher said:

"Why, Captain, I don't have any persuasion with the few men who room at my place. I never tell a man where to sign on."

"Come, come, Kelly," Porter replied. "Let's not spar with each other. Your reputation is known as far as Liverpool. I need a good seaman, and I need him tonight. Can you get one?"

"Well, Captain, for $200 American, I might be able to get you a man," said Kelly.

"Two hundred dollars! Why, that's twice your usual rate. That's piracy!"

"Well now, Captain," said Bunco. "I believe it's called something else, but the penalty is just as stiff. 'Tis me takin' the chances, and this is a rush order. No matter, though. The choice is yours."

Captain Porter eventually agreed to Bunco's terms: $100 in advance, and another $100 when Kelly delivered a man. Captain Porter returned to his ship, while Kelly drank a toast to his good fortune with a friend, saloon keeper Stingaree Poe, often a henchman in procuring men for ship's crews. After downing several healthy belts of rum, Kelly and Poe began the rounds of saloons and hangouts, looking for a seaman. But, they could find no sailor willing to sign on the *Warwick*, or drunk enough not to be wary of Bunco Kelly. At each place they stopped, they spent a little more of Captain Porter's advance money, so that by late evening they were three sheets to the wind, as sailors are known to remark.

As the pair weaved down a Portland street, still looking for a seaman, Kelly suddenly stopped, and said:

"Wait a minute, Poe. Who's that over there?"

Stingaree stared through the rain, then laughed:

"Why, that's Wildman's Cigar Store Indian. Don't think Captain Porter would want him for his crew!"

But, Kelly's bleary mind was working. He said:

"Well, now, 'spose the good captain didn't find out who it was 'til he got to sea? What could he do then?"

And, so, with great effort, Bunco Kelly and Stingaree Poe managed to get rubber boots and a Sou'wester hat on the wooden Indian. Then they covered it with sailor's oilskins and hauled it up the gangway of the *Warwick*. While Captain Porter went for the rest of the money, Kelly and Poe stowed the new crew man below deck, and covered him with blankets. Then they met the captain back on deck. Kelly said:

"Well, Captain, he's stiff as a board right now. I'd let him stay below deck until you're past Astoria. Then he'll stand up with the best of them — I'll guarantee that. Yes, siree, once he gets up, he'll be strong as your mainmast."

So, thanks to Bunco Kelly, that is how a cigar store Indian went "down to the sea in ships." Or, maybe it was down to the sea in *chips* when Captain Porter discovered the charade.

A BUMP IN THE GLOVE

Wagons had gathered in St. Joseph, Missouri, in April, 1846, getting ready for the long and arduous journey to Oregon country. Holding the reins of one team was a diminutive lady, whose blue eyes were wide with excitement below steel-grey hair. She was Tabitha Moffat Brown, a widow, then 66 years old. Beside Tabitha sat Captain John Brown, nearly 80 years old, the brother of her late husband. As their wagon was guided into line, Orus Brown, leader of the train, rode up and said:

"Well, Mother, we're ready to go. Sure this is what you want to do? This trip won't be like a buggy ride down the streets of St. Joe!"

Tabitha Brown assured her son that hundreds of miles of prairie, rugged mountains, unbridged rivers and hostile Indians were not going to stop HER from going to Oregon. And, what's more, Uncle John would make it, too. The set of her chin told Orus as much as her words.

All went fine with the wagon train past Fort Hall, Idaho, still 800 miles from their Oregon destination. Then, trouble slowed the train. Food supplies were short, and the crisp days of autumn forewarned the coming of winter. Orus Brown put his brother-in-law, Virgil Pringle, in charge of the train and rode ahead to seek food and assistance. But, after Brown left the train, Pringle and the other men were convinced that a short-cut across the desert would get them to the Willamette Valley faster than the usual Columbia River route. They moved out on what later was to be called the Scott-Applegate Trail, through Nevada and a corner of northern California into southern Oregon. The party suffered much hardship along the way, including having to give up most of their possessions and many wagons. Gradually, members of the train began parting company, with some wagons moving ahead, others following at a slower pace. One day Virgil Pringle told Tabitha Brown:

"We're going to have to stop to rest and feed the cattle. You and Uncle John take these good horses, and try to catch up with the Thompsons. They can't be too far ahead. Good luck, and God bless you!"

So, with the ailing Captain Brown, Tabitha struck out alone in the wilderness of southern Oregon, with only three slices of bacon and half a cup of tea for nourishment. She feared John Brown might not live through the first night. But, fortune was with the spunky grandmother, for two days later she and her companion were met by members of the original party. And, though near starvation for the next few days, they arrived on Christmas at the home of a Methodist minister in Salem. The minister later recalled:

"Mrs. Brown told me she felt an object in the end of a glove finger, that she assumed was a button. When she checked, she found it was a 6 1/4 cent piece. 'Not much to start a new life with,' she said. 'But, I guess it will have to do!'"

Well, with that coin, Tabitha Brown bought two needles and some thread. Then she traded some of her dresses to an Indian woman for buckskins. She worked those skins into fine gloves for ladies and gentlemen in Salem, and before long had the start of a fair nest egg. Tabitha also accepted the invitation of friends to spend the rest of the winter at Tualatin Plains, now Forest Grove. There, with donations from many pioneers, she started a home for orphans and a day school for other children in the area.

Eventually, Tabitha Brown's day school became a boarding school and staff and programs were added to its curriculum. And, in 1854, the Territorial Legislature granted a charter to that educational institution, which since has become known as Pacific University — a school that can trace its beginnings to the tenacious lady with a bump in her glove.

HALL JACKSON KELLY — PROPHET OF OREGON

One of the most energetic promoters for the settling of Oregon country early in the last century was a New Englander who had never set foot west of the Mississippi.

Hall Jackson Kelly, a visionary author, first became interested in Oregon from his readings of the journals of Lewis & Clark, in 1807. By 1818 he had conceived a plan for colonization of a new republic of civil and religious freedom on the shores of the Pacific. Kelly wrote:

"I have the strong belief that the vast region of Oregon country must at some remote period become of great importance to our government and it will be of deep and general interest. Oregon eventually will become a favorite field of modern enterprise and the abode of civilization. I'll devote my life to realization of my plan."

Kelly was an informed and persuasive man. He read everything he could find about the Oregon country, and, in turn, wrote extensively of the beauty and the commercial potential of the land beyond the mountains. His books and pamphlets extolled the virtues of Oregon, and he even developed a prospectus that included a city at the confluence of the Columbia and Willamette Rivers — even though he still had not come west himself.

Finally, in 1829, Hall Jackson Kelly organized the American Society for Encouraging Settlement of the Oregon Territory. He issued a manual on the Oregon expedition and a book titled, A GEOGRAPHICAL SKETCH OF THAT PART OF NORTH AMERICA CALLED OREGON. And he announced:

"I am forming two expeditions to go to Oregon by wagon train. The first will start on January 1, 1832. That will be just for men. The second will consist of men and their families. There will be many hardships, but all will be worth it when we reach Oregon."

Kelly postponed the expedition while petitioning Congress for aid, and eventually his plans disintegrated, although a number of settlers did join Nathanial Wyeth's wagon train for Oregon in 1832. Kelly himself set out for Oregon by way of New Orleans and Mexico, and had the misfortune of joining a band of men accused of stealing horses, unbeknownst to Kelly. He also contracted malaria. When he finally arrived at Fort Vancouver, he was penniless, ill and unwelcome, for word of the horse thievery had preceded him.

Kelly was given food and shelter by Dr. John McLoughlin, chief factor of the Hudson's Bay Company, but beyond that McLoughlin and others at Fort Vancouver would have nothing to do with the American. Even Wyeth, whom Kelly had inflamed with the desire to go to Oregon, stayed away from Kelly because of the accusations. Wyeth later wrote:

"I was astonished to find Kelly at Fort Vancouver. He arrived with a group that had stolen some horses from the settlers in California. In fact, General Figueroa, the governor of California, wrote Dr. McLoughlin to have no dealings with him. Oh, he has been given a house, and he gets food from McLoughlin's table, but he has not been received as a gentleman."

When his health returned, Kelly was given passage to the Sandwich Islands. Eventually he returned to New England, where he continued to write of the need to colonize the Oregon country, and to petition Congress. And, though he died in seclusion, with few persons aware of his contribution to the settlement of the western lands, his efforts were not overlooked by historians. Editor Harvey W. Scott wrote:

"Kelly was an eccentric man — an enthusiast — one of those who sees a single idea and devotes his life to it. But he was the first to urge settlement of Oregon and to recognize its importance to the United States. Many with whom he came in contact regarded him merely as a bore or troublesome fellow. I say this strange eccentric man can almost be called a Prophet of Oregon, the father of migration to Oregon and the man who hastened the fulfillment of Oregon's destiny."

THE S.S. BEAVER

Oregon is called the Beaver state for good reason, as the prized pelt of this ambitious rodent was in great part responsible for the first journeys into the vast territory of the northwest. So, it is not unusual to find the name "Beaver" on some of the ships used in the fur trade.

One Beaver that stands alone in the annals of maritime history is the *S.S. Beaver*, an English vessel that was the first steamship in the Pacific Ocean and the inland waters of the northwestern territories. The *Beaver* actually was the first steam vessel to cross the Atlantic and to go around Cape Horn, but as a naval historian once pointed out:

"Technically, that is true, but mind you, she did not cross the Atlantic or 'round the Horn under steam. No, *Beaver* crossed the ocean under sail, and also sailed around the Horn. But, once in Oregon, she did, indeed, use steam propulsion."

The *Beaver* was commissioned in England in 1834 by the Hudson's Bay Company. Because the ship was being built at a time when many problems of marine steam propulsion were yet to be solved, she created untold interest in the world's ship-building circles and public alike. Considerable interest was shown in the Royal Palace, for King William IV loved the sea and all things nautical. In fact, when the *Beaver* was launched in the Thames River in May, 1835, King William announced:

"This is a day that opens a new era in both frontier discovery and world trade. I shall attend the launching, and I hereby decree that the Royal courts shall adjourn for the day so that all members of the family and the court who wish to witness this historic launching may do so."

So, from this notable beginning, *Beaver's* course was charted to the New World, her paddle wheel safely stowed in a hold for fear of the ravaging waves of the Atlantic and Cape Horn. The ship stood into the Columbia River on March 19, 1836, and after a short stay at the colony of Astoria, set sail once again for the Hudson's Bay post at Fort Vancouver.

At Fort Vancouver, intense interest was again expressed in the small ship, for now her carpenters and engineers were to finish their task by installing the paddle wheel and testing her engines. Skeptics thought the paddle wheel would not be able to withstand the river's current, or that it might be torn apart by wayward logs. But, the *Beaver* made her trial run down the Columbia to the mouth of the Willamette River with perfection, and was judged ready for immediate service. So, on June 26, 1836, the ship that had entered the Columbia under sail, now chugged back to Astoria and the Pacific Ocean under her own power. And, for the next half-century, *Beaver* was a familiar sight along the northwest coast, where she was referred to as the "little black steamer." *Beaver* was used as a trader, explorer, freighter, Royal Navy vessel, tow boat and hydrographic surveyor, and in that role charted 900 miles of the northwest coast to Alaska.

After the *Beaver* was sold to a towboat company by the Hudson's Bay Company in 1874, a curse seemed to follow the once-useful vessel. Fire nearly destroyed the ship in 1880, though she was repaired and returned to service. In 1883, she struck a rock in Burrards Inlet, and sank. Once again she was restored and recommissioned. But, when she ran aground on rocks at the entrance to the Vancouver, B.C., harbor in 1888, little effort was made to salvage her. Eventually, she washed away to a watery grave in the Pacific.

Despite the ignoble end, *Beaver* had left her mark. As one historian said:

"I believe we must agree on one thing. The *Beaver* was aptly named, for this was a working vessel, not a legendary one — just like her namesake."

WHITEAKER'S RIDE

To John Whiteaker, a pro-slavery Democrat with secessionist leanings, belongs the distinction of being the first governor of the State of Oregon. Curiously, Whiteaker, took the oath of office seven months before the U.S. Congress acted to make Oregon a state! So, for a brief period, Oregon had two governors: State Governor John Whiteaker and Territorial Governor George L. Curry, who, incidentally, kept right on "governoring" after Whiteaker's election until President Buchanan signed Oregon's statehood bill in early 1859.

The mix-up of governors came about because of the slowness of transportation and communication in the 1850's. Believing that Congress had enacted an Oregon statehood bill, the people in the Territory held an election for state officers in the summer of 1858 and inaugurated Whiteaker on July 8. To their surprise the Oregonians learned later that the bill had not yet passed through Congress. Governor-elect Whiteaker yielded to Governor Curry until the matter was settled. Whiteaker assumed office on March 9, 1859.

So, it was Whiteaker who was in office when Fort Sumter was fired on, launching America into the Civil War. Whiteaker ignored President Abraham Lincoln's proclamation for 75,000 troops to help put down the revolution. Instead, the Oregon governor said:

"Because the people of this state come from every section of the country, it would certainly be impolitic of us, however keenly we may sympathize with other sections, to subject ourselves to the calamities which afflict them."

Despite the governor's objections, many Oregonians did volunteer for service in the Union army. For that matter, other Oregonians volunteered for the Confederate army, confirming Whiteaker's opinion.

But, it was not John Whiteaker's anti-war statements and pro-slavery sympathies that brought him nationwide attention in the last century. After leaving the governor's office, Whiteaker served in the Oregon legislature, and then was elected to the U.S. House of Representatives in 1878. Business interests kept him from getting started to Washington for the opening of the 49th Congress in March, 1879, and the Democratic leaders of the House realized they needed one more vote to elect a Speaker of the House favorable to their program. One said:

"We've got to get that extra vote. Now, that man Whiteaker, from Oregon, is not here yet. We've got to locate him and see that he gets here before the vote."

By then, John Whiteaker had left Oregon on the steamship *Elder*. And, when the ship dropped anchor in San Francisco Bay, an agent for the Central Pacific Railroad came aboard and told the new Congressman that a special train awaited him at the Oakland terminal. It had been chartered by the Democratic National Committee, to get him to the capitol as quickly as possible. Whiteaker was rowed ashore immediately to the San Francisco ferry terminal, where a ferryboat was waiting to take him across the bay to Oakland. A short time later he was speeding eastward. Whiteaker, in recalling the trip later, told friends:

"Well, that so-called train consisted of a locomotive and a coach, and the engineer had been forbidden to stop even for a decent meal. I had to subsist on some canned goods for four days and 20 hours. Why it was nearly enough to make a Republican of me!"

But, John Whiteaker did arrive in Washington the morning of March 18, and that very day cast the deciding ballot for the Speaker of the House. And, while his coast-to-coast trip of 116 hours seems like an eternity in this era of space-age travel, at the time it was a record crossing, and at a cost of $1,500 to the sponsors who needed his vote.

THE BING CHERRY

Many experts at the 1876 Centennial Exposition in Philadelphia were shocked when an orchardist from the faraway state of Oregon won the world's premium for the finest pears and cherries, particularly since the fruit had been shipped across the country.

But, they shouldn't have been surprised, for the fruit was the treasure of Seth Lewelling, a horticulturist on a par with Burbank, though without the national reputation of the latter. Lewelling, with his brother, Henderson, had much to do with the development and growth of the fruit industry in Oregon. Both men had learned the trade from their father, a physician and nurseryman who had established orchards in Indiana and Iowa.

It was Henderson Lewelling who first decided to move to Oregon in 1847, taking with him 700 sapling fruit trees. A friend told him:

"Henderson, I can't for the life of me see why you want to leave Iowa. You've established a good business, and have all the land a man possibly could need. 'Sides, how do you think you're going to get all those trees to Oregon? Why, *people* die out there on the trail for lack of water. Think what will happen to those little trees."

But, Henderson was determined, and it took him nearly six months to make the overland journey from Salem, Iowa to newly-founded Milwaukie, where he started a nursery. Only about one-half his fruit stock survived the trip, yet legend has it that the trees at one point saved Henderson and the wagon train from peril. When hostile Indians prepared to attack the train, they noticed the boxes of trees, some in bloom, carried in Lewelling's wagon. The Indians decided Lewelling was a great medicine man and allowed the train to pass.

Seth Lewelling joined his brother in Milwaukie a short time after Henderson arrived in Oregon, and within a few years they had grafted thousands of fruit trees for sale to other settlers in the Willamette Valley. Some historians say Seth was the true horticulturist and Henderson the promoter, but in any case, they were a viable team. Seth constantly experimented with new varieties of fruit, originating the Golden prune, Sweet Alice apple, Mother's Favorite pear, and the favored Lincoln and Black Republican cherries. Of the last variety, the staunch Quaker abolitionist joked:

"Some of the copperheads around here like to call *me* a black republican because of my religion and my politics. But, I tell you, I'm going to make them relish the Black Republican!"

Actually, it is another of Seth Lewelling's cherries that came to be savored more than either the Lincoln or the Black Republican. When a large, succulent table variety matured in about 1875, the question of a name was discussed. Finally Seth Lewelling said:

"Those cherries came from Bing's row. Now, Bing was a big man, and that is a big cherry, so we'll just call it the Bing cherry."

Bing, a stalwart Manchu from Northern China, was Seth Lewelling's superintendent, who had worked side by side with the nurseryman for more than 30 years. By unfortunate chance, Bing had returned to his homeland to visit his family when the Oriental exclusion act went into effect, and he was prevented from returning to America. But today, a century since its development, Oregon's Bing cherry still is a favorite and a lasting honor to the man who made it grow.

JESSE BOONE AND HIS ROAD

Portland was little more than a few shacks when Jesse Boone and his brother, Alphonso, settled on the Willamette River in 1844, and began carrying passengers across the river in a canoe. But, one day Alphonso told Jesse:

"Jesse, folks are talking about finding gold in California. We could carry people across this river for the next hundred years and not make the coin that a gold strike would bring us."

So, the Boone brothers set out for California, the dreams of riches in their minds. But, industrious Jesse Boone was not a miner at heart, and before long he was back in Portland, telling people of a plan:

"I'm going to build a road south to the Willamette, and then I'll put in a ferry that can haul wagons and stock across the river. It won't be long now before there is trade between Portland and the new cities in the valley."

Jesse Boone, a grandson of the noted Kentucky frontiersman, Daniel Boone, hacked a road out of the timber and thickets from Portland to a location 16 miles south on the Willamette River. There, in 1847, he launched a ferry boat that became of untold benefit to travellers and tradesmen in the Willamette Valley. For the next quarter of a century he criss-crossed the river with increasing frequency as people moved to Oregon. But, in 1872, an argument took place at the ferry, and Jesse Boone was shot and killed by a neighbor, Joseph Engle. Another neighbor reported at that time:

"I don't know for sure what started the fight between Jesse and Joe Engle, but I think Joe thought Jesse was overcharging him on the ferry. Don't seem right, though. Jesse was an honest and decent man, and I can't imagine him cheating anybody."

Joseph Engle was tried and convicted of second degree murder for killing Jesse Boone, and was sentenced to life imprisonment in April, 1872. His term was short, though, for he died of typhoid fever the following July. And, though Jesse Boone no longer was at the helm, his boat continued to service the commerce and pleasure travel in the Willamette Valley, tying in with the river boats that then steamed up and down the river.

Even after the railroads put an end to river boats on the Willamette, the daily runs of the ferry were continued. When the town of Wilsonville was established at the southern end of the road Jesse Boone had cleared out of the wilderness, the ferry became known as the Wilsonville Ferry. But, after a modern highway bridge was stretched across the Willamette in 1954, ferry service was discontinued at that point of the river.

However, the legacy of Jesse Boone lives on, for Boones Ferry Road is a paved thoroughfare that winds through suburbs and farm lands from Portland to the Willamette River, serving the needs of modern travellers just as it did our Oregon ancestors more than a century ago.

BENJAMIN STARK, PORTLAND PIONEER

A small group of citizens had gathered for the town meeting in the new settlement called Portland in the early 1850's, and they were engaged in a heated argument about the need for public schools. One man said:

"Now Mr. Stark, here you are the epitome of an educated man, yet you're arguing against the school. Surely you want the same opportunity for your children — and mine — that you had?"

Benjamin Stark, witty, urbane and practical, answered:

"Indeed, Sir, indeed I do. But you misunderstand my remarks and my intent. I am by no means against education, and I do not deny the need for a school. Our greatest need at the this time is for a jail. The taxpayers can't afford both a jailhouse and a schoolhouse, and since we seem to have in our midst more scoundrels than scholars, I say we must opt for the jail."

Stark's opinion prevailed, and it was several years before a public school was founded in Portland. And, it seems apparent why Benjamin Stark was able to influence others. A descendent of New England stock, Stark was an intelligent and somewhat affluent businessman who had gone to New York at the age of 15, and within 10 years had established a thriving merchandising business that included trade between Portland and the Sandwich Islands. In fact, Stark was in charge of the ship that brought news to Oregon that England had signed the treaty making Oregon country the sole possession of the United States. That word had been relayed via the Sandwich Islands, and was brought to the new territory by Benjamin Stark himself. As to his personal demeanor, a friend once said:

"Ben Stark is a strict churchman, and is possessed of that greatest of all gifts — charity. He has a charming personality, and is many-sided — well-informed, perfect of memory, genial, and courtly in the way of the old school. He is liked by men who are both his junior and who lead him in age. Yes, I would say of Ben that he is the potent example of the Christian gentleman."

Stark had come to Portland in 1845, to settle on a donation land claim that later was to become a prominent portion of downtown Portland. Considerable litigation was concerned with his land during the first decade he owned it. In 1850, he gave up his business to study law, and was admitted to the bar. He rose rapidly in public life, and was elected a member of the Territorial Legislature. Then, in 1861, Stark was appointed U.S. Senator to fill the term of Colonel E.D. Baker, who had been killed in a Civil War battle. When that term was over, in 1863, Stark moved his family to New London, Connecticut, where he had spent his youth. There he remained the rest of his days, though he did make occasional trips to Oregon to check on his property holdings. A friend once recalled:

"Senator Stark was part of New England's best and most progressive life. He was a Democrat by principle, and was a consistent and honest supporter of the politics of his party. He frequently was elected to city offices, and represented New London in the Connecticut General Assembly. He believed in the future of New London, and labored for it with all his heart."

And, though Mr. Stark had opposed the construction of a school in Portland, he spent 24 years as a member of the board of education in New London. Upon his death, in 1898, a New London newspaper opined:

"Mr. Stark was a lover of our public schools and he gave valuable assistance to their care and development. His voice and his vote could be counted on for every retrograde movement. It is difficult to estimate the debt New London owes to him for his conscientious services in the department of public education alone."

Well, Benjamin Stark left Portland a street, if not a school, for Stark Street is a major thoroughfare that stretches through the southern sector of the city, east from the land he once owned toward the New England of his birth — and burial.

THE MYSTERY OF SHIP J.C. COUSINS

October 7, 1883 dawned clear on the Oregon coast. The ocean was flat, and a moderate ground swell was running off the mouth of the Columbia River. Outside the Columbia Bar, the pilot boat *J.C. Cousins*, an 87-foot, two-masted topsail schooner, was cruising the calm Pacific at full sail.

A man on watch in the tower at Ft. Stevens held a long glass on the ship, envious of her freedom on the high seas. Suddenly he shouted:

"Hey, look! Something's wrong on the *Cousins*. She's headin' right for Clatsop Spit, and she's still under full sail."

As men at Ft. Stevens and the nearby Pt. Adams Coast Guard Station watched, the schooner sailed headlong for the beach, her canvas still unfurled. Suddenly, the graceful craft lurched violently as her copperclad hull smashed over a shoal. Now she was firmly aground. Breakers began washing over her decks, beginning an unremitting pounding of the vessel. At Pt. Adams, an alarm was sounded, and trained seamen readied two longboats. An officer wondered:

"Why don't they use their lifeboats? I haven't seen a flare or any other distress signal. What's going on out there, anyway? Captain Zeiber knows this coastline as well as anyone."

Life-saving boats rowed to the *Cousins*, now held in a death grip by the sand. Still the ship's sails had not been hauled down, and her whipping canvas snapped like rifle shots in the stiffening breeze. As the launches approached the *Cousins*, the Coast Guard seamen hailed the ship. No one answered.

The first men over the side of the foundering schooner discovered the *Cousins* deserted, though everything seemed in order. Lines were coiled, gear stashed, bunks lashed up. Her galley stove was still warm to the touch, and a pot of potatoes had boiled dry. But nowhere — not in the cabin, the wheelhouse, chain storage or crews quarters — was there any sign of Captain Alonzo Zeiber or his crew of three men. A petty officer told the lieutenant in charge of the Coast Guard detail:

"Lieutenant, I've got in 26 years, and I've never seen anything like this. Somebody's been watching this ship since sunrise, and we ain't seen anybody jump off or leave in any other way. And look — here, in the wheelhouse. See that ashtray? Those are cigar ashes, and they were still smoldering when we came aboard. I'm telling you, somebody steered that ship onto the spit. But, where did he go?"

A thorough investigation of the wreck turned up no clues. The *Cousins*, fitted out originally as a luxury yacht, had been brought to Astoria from San Francisco in 1881. She was put in service as a Columbia River Bar pilot craft, opening a rate-cutting war with rival pilot services. The skipper of the *Cousins*, Alonzo Zeiber, was a skilled mariner, as were the men of his crew.

The *Cousins* had sailed from Astoria the day before the wreck, and had spent some time in the Columbia River before crossing the bar and remaining at sea for the night. Since daybreak she had been watched by the men on shore. The last entry in her log was at dawn, and indicated "all's well."

In the weeks following the wreck, beachcombers from Oregon's Tillamook Head to Washington's Dead Man's Hollow patrolled the sands day and night, waiting for the corpses they expected to wash ashore. None did.

Ultimately, the *Cousins* was claimed by the sea, for the ship could not be refloated, and winter storms smashed her to pieces. A marine insurance company paid her owners $4,000, a mere 10 cents on the dollar, to settle the bewitching claim.

What happened to the captain and the crew of the *J.C. Cousins*? One theory was that the captain had been bribed by rival pilots to murder his crew and sink their bodies, then destroy his ship. But Zeiber and his men were known to be close associates who had often spent time together ashore at Astoria. In the near century since the *Cousins* was dashed to cordwood on the Pacific breakers, no one has solved the mystery. None of the crew was seen again. Like many riddles of the deep, this one has many questions — but no answers.

FIRST CLIMB OF MT. HOOD

To the first party of white men climbing the snow-covered slopes of Mt. Hood in 1854, the peak seemed much higher than it really is. At one point, Thomas Jefferson Dryer, Portland newspaper editor and leader of the expedition, said:

"This air is thinner than I had imagined. We must have climbed at least 18,000 feet, and we're not near the top yet."

Though Dryer was considerably off in his estimate of the height of the 11,245-foot peak, he was not off in his claim to be the first white man to climb the mountain. Nor was this his first such claim, for Dryer had made the initial climb of Mt. St. Helens the year before.

To Dryer, the Hood climb was both an outdoor adventure and relief from the bitter political feuds of the day. And, as editor of what is now Oregon's oldest newspaper, *The Oregonian*, Dryer could give his readers an eye-witness account of the deed. Considering the lack of proper equipment and knowledge of the mountain, it was daring.

Dryer was accompanied by a French sea captain, T.O. Travailliot, when he rode out of Portland on August 4, 1854. They rode their horses to Foster's homestead, on Eagle Creek, a noted stopping point for travellers on the famous Barlow Road, where they spent the first night. There Dryer and Travailliot were joined by Wells Lake and Captain William Barlow, son of the trailblazer for whom the pioneer road through the Cascade Mountains was named.

The next day, August 5, the party of four men rode 30 miles to the base of Mt. Hood. But, on the third day, the going was rougher, for only primitive game trails provided a path through forest thickets. Dryer estimated they covered only six miles that third day, though Captain Travailliot commented it seemed more like 60! At a snow line camp that night, Dryer built signal fires for Judge Cyrus Olney, of The Dalles, who was to meet them on the mountain.

The following morning, Judge Olney, accompanied by Army Major Granville O. Haller and an Indian guide, found the campsite. Shortly thereafter, a fierce storm forced the climbers to move around to the southeast side of the mountain, where they made camp in a beautiful meadow. At dusk, Judge Olney studied the mountain with his small telescope, and said:

"Tom, look through this scope. I distinctly see smoke coming from the extreme top of the mountain. See what you see."

This discovery increased Thomas Dryer's determination to reach the top, for until then, Mt. Hood had not generally been considered to be of volcanic origin. Early the next morning, August 8, 1854, the men rode as far up the slope as they could, then picketed their horses. Captain Barlow volunteered to stay with the animals, as the others began their climbing assault. When they started out, each climber went his own way, but after two hours, realized the mistake of this approach and decided to keep together. Soon they were climbing an ice floe Dryer reported to be of an incline of 50 degrees. Major Haller dropped out because of dizziness, and then Captain Travailliot and Judge Olney could go no further because of the steepness of the slope. Before reaching the top, the three remaining climbers — Thomas Dryer, Wells Lake and their unidentified Indian guide — came upon a rocky area of many volcanic fissures, or fumaroles, from which hot smoke and gas were escaping. Dryer later reported that when the guide discovered the existence of fire below, he retreated down the mountain. But, Dryer and Lake pushed on. At 2:50 p.m. they reached the summit and enjoyed the vista for hundreds of miles around the mountain, a view now familiar to the thousands who have since followed those pioneer climbers to the top of the mountain.

THE BULLDOG OF THE FLEET

Ships make history in a variety of ways. Some for their sleek beauty, some for their power, some for their exploits and the valor of the crew. A vessel memorialized for all of those reasons was the *U.S.S. Oregon,* one of the first armor-clad battleships designed to help build the United States into a sea power.

The *Oregon* was built in San Francisco in the 1890's, proving once and for all that major ships could be constructed on the Pacific coast, away from the steel centers of the eastern United States. Her massive rudder was the largest casting then made on the coast.

From the beginning, the *Oregon* floated on a sea of pride and confidence, and such an attitude was justified soon after her initial shake down cruises. The ship was just completing a routine overhaul at Bremerton when America was shocked by the news of the destruction of the *U.S.S. Maine* in the harbor at Havana, Cuba. The *Oregon* steamed immediately to San Francisco, where she was made ready for a long voyage. On March 18, 1898, she sailed from the harbor of her christening, under sealed orders, on what proved to be the most renowned cruise in naval history to that time. Once underway, Captain Charles E. Clark told his officers:

"Gentlemen, we have all speculated as to our destination — whether we would join Dewey in the Philippines, or Admiral Sampson in Cuba. My orders are to take the *Oregon,* with all speed, to Key West, Florida, where we will join the Atlantic Fleet."

For the next ten weeks, the 12,000-ton juggernaut steamed with bulldog determination through unbearable equatorial heat and gale-blown seas, stopping only to restock provisions and coal in South American ports. Fresh water was rationed so that it could be used in the ship's boilers, to prevent possible fouling with sea water and a slowing of her speed. On May 26, 1898, the *Oregon* arrived at Key West, having made her 14,500 mile trip in the unheard of time of 71 days. The *Oregon* proved her design was sound, but she demonstrated dramatically the need for a canal in the Panama Isthmus. When Captain Clark reported to Admiral Sampson, he was told:

"Captain, your achievement was remarkable. But, take your ship into port. She must need an overhaul after that trip."

"No, Admiral, she does not," Clark responded. "We came here to fight, and we are ready."

Less than three days later, the *Oregon* was once again at sea, this time with her course set for Cuba and the Santiago Harbor, where the American navy had bottled up the Spanish fleet. When the Spanish ships finally steamed out, under cover of heavy clouds, battle gongs rang out on the American vessels amid cries of "Remember the *Maine!*" And, when the smoke of the battle cleared away, the American gunners saw the pride and power of Spain sinking and burning along the Cuban coast. The *Oregon,* which fired both the first and last salvos of the fray, had engaged four armored cruisers and two torpedo boats, and received a rousing "Well Done" from Fleet Admiral Sampson. She also earned the reputation "Bulldog of the Fleet" to go with the nickname already bestowed on her.

Well, the "Bulldog" saw service in the Pacific during the Boxer Rebellion and was used again in World War I. Then she was decommissioned and became a floating maritime museum in the harbor at Portland. She was drafted back into service in World War II, and her once-proud hull was turned into an ammunition barge at the island of Guam. In 1956, she was sold for scrap to Japanese investors.

The mast of the "Bulldog of the Fleet" stands as a memorial on the Portland waterfront, and memory of her achievements fade as those who served on her or were familiar with her record pass on. But, perhaps no tribute to the *Oregon* was any higher than that of one of England's noted admirals, Lord Charles Beresford, who once said of *Oregon's* speed run:

"When one of my officers tries to downgrade the achievement of the *Oregon* by saying, 'We have ships that could do it,' I answer, 'Yes, but we have *not* done it. The *Oregon* has.'"

ELLEN SABIN, SUPERINTENDENT

A heated discussion was taking place at an evening meeting of the Portland Board of Education in July, 1888. Finally, the chairman of the board rapped on the table and said:

"Gentlemen, gentlemen. . . please. Let's come to order. You have heard Mr. Ladd's motion that Ellen Sabin be chosen superintendent of schools. Is there additional comment before we vote?"

One member of the board said:

"Mr. Chairman, I don't question Miss Sabin's abilities as an educator. We have seen evidence of that while she has been principal at North School. But, if I may be candid, I question whether a woman, even a capable woman, can handle the complex duties of the superintendent. Why, what does she know about furnaces, and sewer pipes, and the planning of school houses? You will recall Superintendent Crawford's report. He noted that the superintendent must be a 'man of all work.'"

Despite chauvinistic attitudes and objections by some members of the board, Ellen C. Sabin was elected superintendent of schools in Portland, the first woman to hold such a position in any major city in the United States. And, what a choice for Portland! An innovative educator, Ellen Sabin had grown up in Wisconsin and was educated at the University of Wisconsin, although not granted a degree, since the University did not grant degrees to women at that time. After teaching in her hometown of Sun Prairie, and later Madison, Miss Sabin moved west with her family in the 1870's. She established a school in Eugene, where her family settled, and then applied for a job as a teacher in Portland three years later when her father moved the rest of the family back to Wisconsin. After teaching one year at North School in Portland, she was offered the position of principal, much to the concern of other principals in the city, for she was the first woman to have such a job in Portland. The annual salary of $1,800 for a principal was cut to $1,600 for the young Miss Sabin because of her "being a female!"

North School was located near the waterfront, and drew children from an area lined with taverns and dirty wharves. Miss Sabin was concerned not only with the learning environment of the children at school, but with their personal cleanliness and attitude. She frequently went out at night, alone, to discuss a problem with a child's parents — often carrying laundry soap and a delousing prescription, both of which she encouraged parents to use. Friends did not like her being unaccompanied on her sojourns into rough neighborhoods. But, one day the police chief said:

"Miss Sabin, I can tell you're not going to stay out of those areas. I can't guarantee your safety, but I can do this. I'm giving you an official police badge, and I want you to wear it when you're out. People respect the law, and I think you'll be left alone."

Once she was elected to the joint position of superintendent and principal of Central High School in 1888, Ellen Sabin wasted no time starting programs she considered important to the city. She established the first public kindergartens, and initiated the first night school classes — for girls, only. Grades were renumbered from a complicated code system to the logical progression of first through eighth. She also abolished the practice of final examinations as the sole basis for promotion to a higher grade.

Though Miss Sabin was recognized as a successful innovator and educational practitioner, the school board decided not to rehire her as superintendent when her contract expired in 1890. But, Miss Sabin already had been invited to take the presidency of Donner College, in her native Wisconsin. When Donner merged with Milwaukee Woman's College in 1895, she continued as president, a position she held until her retirement in 1921.

Ellen Sabin lived until the year 1949, and was 98 years old when she died. Her legacy to Portland lives on, though not, curiously, through Sabin Grade School, which was named instead for her *brother*, Robert Sabin, a former member of the Portland School Board.

SALT OF THE SEA

Christmas Day, 1805. The men of the Lewis and Clark Expedition exchanged meager gifts, shouted, fired shots from their muzzle-loaders, and sang Christmas songs at their small stockade at Fort Clatsop, near the mouth of the Columbia River.

But, it was not the merriest Christmas for those hardy adventurers, who had crossed half the North American continent to explore the northwest and the "Great River of the West." Captain William Clark, co-leader of the party, later wrote:

"We would have spent this Christmas Day in feasting had we anything to either raise our spirits or gratify our appetites. Our dinner consisted of poor elk, so much spoiled that we ate it through mere necessity. We also had some spoiled pounded fish and a few roots ..."

It seems almost bizarre that the explorers, situated as they were in a land of plentiful game and fish, had trouble with their provisions. But, they lacked an important quantity, salt, an item the friendly coastal Indians could not provide. To make their monotonous diet more palatable, and to preserve food for their return journey, they needed the mineral. On December 28, five men were dispatched to the sea shore to find a suitable place where they could boil sea water. The spot they selected was about 15 miles south of Fort Clatsop, a short distance back from the ocean and about one-half mile from the Necanicum River. Nearby were Clatsop and Tillamook Indian villages, and the Indians helped the white men build a crude rock cairn, shaped like a horseshoe, about eight feet long. Wood stacked around the piled rocks provided enough heat to boil sea water in five kettles the men had hauled from Fort Clatsop.

On January 5, 1806, Peter Wiser and some of the other salt makers returned to the stockade. Wiser reported:

"We're bilin' salt water day'n night. Reckon as how we're gettin' 'bout a gallon o' salt a day, now. Here, I brought some back for you to try."

The fine, white salt was welcomed by Meriwether Lewis, who wrote in his journal:

"It was a great day for myself and most of the party — I say most of the party, because my friend, Captain Clark, declared it to be a mere matter of indifference to him whether he uses salt or not. For myself, I must confess I felt a considerable inconvenience from the want of it. The want of bread I consider trivial, provided I get fat meat. And for the species of meat I am not particular, whether the flesh of the dog or the horse or the wolf, having from habit become easily familiar as with any other. I have learned to think that if the cord be sufficiently strong, which binds the soul and body together, it does not much matter about the materials which compose it."

The saltmakers worked until late February, when they returned to Fort Clatsop with about 20 gallons of the seasoning. Preparations then were underway for the long journey east. On March 23, 1806, Lewis and Clark presented their stockade to Chief Cobaway of the Clatsops and the men started back up the Columbia.

That crude salt cairn, so important to the men of the Lewis and Clark Expedition, was all but forgotten for nearly a hundred years, and the town of Seaside grew up around it. About the turn of the century, historians located the cairn, and eventually a fence was erected around it. The Seaside Lions Club rebuilt the stone formation to make it as representative as possible of the one used by those original saltmakers, and the site was donated to the Oregon Historical Society by landowners. Today, the Lewis and Clark Salt Cairn is visited by thousands of persons annually — most of whom take for granted that salt *always* came from the boxes available at a nearby store.

LIGE COALMAN, MOUNTAIN CLIMBER

The base of Mt. Hood was home for Elijah Coalman, or Lige Coalman as he was better known, for many years of his extended life. And, while the base might have been home, Lige was just as comfortable on the slopes of the mountain, for during a 23-year span that he lived and worked on the mountain, he climbed to the summit 586 times, a feat recorded in Ripley's *Believe It or Not.*

Lige was the son of Oregon pioneer Stephen Coalman, who in the 1850's had homesteaded near what is now Sandy. Lige left home at the age of 17, and when he returned to settle on the mountain's skirts 13 months later, he had had experience as a hobo, railroad worker, waterfront laborer and boilermaker's helper. It wasn't that young Lige couldn't hold a job: his restless youth pulled him to other things. It also drew him back to the mountain he loved, and to a job as a guide and forest ranger.

Lige Coalman had first climbed Mt. Hood at the age of 15, when he accompanied mountain guide Oliver Yocum to the summit. He later became Yocum's assistant, and eventually took over Yokum's business. Lige was the first man to make a successful winter climb to the top of Hood, and pioneered several routes up the mountain. Over the years he was involved in numerous rescues of injured climbers, and is credited personally with saving the lives of five persons who might have died on the mountain.

One of Coalman's jobs with the forest service was that of fire lookout, stationed at the top of Mt. Hood, where he built a summit cabin in 1915. It was from this vantage point on the mountain's top that he often assisted climbers in trouble. And, it was during this period that Lige would fairly race up and down the mountain, from timberline to the summit. He once made it to the top in 96 minutes, a trip that would take the average climber about six hours.

One time a group witnessed a Coalman mountaineering feat that was related later by a member of the party. He said:

"Well, we were on our way up the mountain, and were resting at the base of Crater Rock, when we saw Lige coming down from the summit. We timed him, and he got to us in about six minutes. Now, normally it takes about an hour to make just that descent. Anyway, he went on down to timberline, picked up some rolls of telephone cable, and began climbing back and laying out wire. He got back to the summit about the same time we did, and fixed some food and tea for us. We were exhausted, but Lige didn't even seem tired!"

Lige Coalman had many narrow escapes on Mt. Hood, any one of which might have claimed his life. He once fell 70 feet into a crevasse, but fortunately landed on soft snow and only sprained his wrists and ankles. Another time, while retrieving the telephone line prior to winter's storms, Lige slipped, and barely caught himself with his feet and legs hanging off a glacier. But, one time, in 1917, while climbing alone from Cloud Cap Chalet to the summit cabin, Lige was caught in a boulder shower. He managed to avoid all but one rock, which struck him in the chest and knocked him unconscious for nearly an hour. Severe chest pains restricted his mountain activities the remainder of that year, and the next summer he had much discomfort while manning the summit lookout.

With his mountaineering limited, Lige Coalman moved his family from Government Camp to Portland in the early 1920's, and turned his energies to church work and the YMCA, including many years at the Y camp at Spirit Lake, Washington. His later years were spent in California, where he continued as a resident director of a YMCA camp until his retirement at age 80.

Lige Coalman lived until 1970, and while he had dreams about ascent number 587, frail health in his final years kept him off the mountain that he had conquered so many times —each with the zeal of a new love. But his record of climbs may never be matched.

A POCKET FULL OF ROCKS

It is hard to imagine a country with no money — or credit cards — for purchase of goods and services, and where each financial transaction is handled by trade. But, that was the situation in Oregon Territory in the 1840's, the beginning of the settlement of the new frontier. Beaver and buckskins, shingles, logs, salmon and hoop poles — all were part of the currency of the day. Minted cash or paper were not to be found. In fact, Col. J.W. Nesmith, Oregon pioneer judge and legislator, once remarked:

"Currency in Oregon Territory was scarcer than hens' teeth, as the saying goes. Why, until about 1848, when we began to see some returns from the California gold mines, there was no *real* money being circulated. Fact is, during the first five years I lived in the territory, the only money I handled was three Mexican dollars."

As gold began filtering back to the territory, it became the medium of exchange, and even led to the minting of the Beaver money in Oregon City. Prior to that time, however, the lack of currency created problems for both shopkeepers and settlers. The Hudson's Bay Company, which had established the first trading posts in the territory, generally controlled the supply of goods in the early days, and provided drawing accounts and credit for purchases. Other stores followed that lead. So, one of the first acts of the Oregon Provisional Legislature, in 1845, was to make the accounts of store orders on solvent merchants a lawful tender, along with gold, silver and U.S. treasury drafts, even though precious metals and treasury drafts were virtually non-existent in the territory.

When George Abernethy acquired the store and stock of goods of the Methodist Mission at the falls of the Willamette, he became the first proprietor to offer solid competition to the Hudson's Bay Company monopoly. But, Abernethy soon found he had a problem. He told a friend:

"You know, trading goods is all right, but it doesn't always come out even. What I need is some fractional money, to make change at the store. It's a bother to me and to my customers to have to carry everything on the books. I've got to figure out *something* that will serve in the place of cash."

Abernethy soon found the answer, in the Indian camp at nearby Willamette Falls. While fishing there for salmon, the Indians passed time making arrowheads and spear points from flint rock. Their work left behind chips of flint in small, thin pieces. One day Abernethy gathered up many of these chips, most about half the size of his thumb. He smoothed and shaped the chips to a size he wanted, then glued slips of tough paper on the chips. On each paper slip he had written the word "change," the year, and the amount each chip was worth. He then added the name "Abernethy" to show that the chips were genuine.

Because of Abernethy's standing in the community, he had no problem gaining acceptance of his rock "change," which was circulated in other businesses as well as his store. Unfortunately, no records show how many Abernethy rock chips were created and circulated, but it is known that the Abernethy rocks are as scarce today as real money was in Oregon Territory those many years ago, In fact, the only known specimen is a grayish piece of flint, marked 35¢, in the collection of the Oregon Historical Society.

But, George Abernethy not only created money. His distribution of the stone chips caused use of the colloquial expression "a pocket full of rocks," which in Oregon meant wealth, and which was used long after flint and skins had been replaced by coin and paper as the medium of exchange.

THE TWO BARS OF BARNEY TRAINOR

To say that an early Portlander named Barney Trainor knew the bar is almost begging the question. For Trainor was Justice of the Peace, and his method of dispensing justice was closely linked to his method of dispensing alcoholic spirits. Judge Trainor, as it happened, also was the owner of the Trainor Hotel in East Portland. The lower part of the hotel was divided: half was the courtroom, and the other half a barroom. Trainor had quite a few methods for catching citizens at one or the other — or both — of his bars. As a crony put it:

"Well, you can bet your baby's highchair, if there's a way to make a dollar, 'ol Barney'll find it. He may be Irish in name, but he's Scotch in nature, to say nothin' of being rich in bourbon."

Though East Portland was sparsely populated in the 1860's, when Judge Trainor held forth, it was a lively community, linked to westside Portland by the Stark Street ferry over the Willamette River. Thus Judge Trainor had frequent business in his two bars. And, if it was slow in one, he'd bring in business from the other. His bartender, a man named Sullivan, also was the east side constable, and no doubt shared in profits from the two bars. It was not uncommon for Sullivan to arrest a man for whom he'd been pouring whiskey on a public drunkenness charge!

One time Judge Trainor witnessed a fight not far from the hotel, and when the combatants were going strong, he summoned Sullivan:

"Sully, there's some business in sight for us. Go up where those young sprigs are fighting, and bring them to court. You might bring along a couple of witnesses, too."

Sullivan did his "duty," and shortly the young men were before the judge's bench. To one, Barney Trainor said:

"You're charged with disturbing the peace. How do you plead?"

"Oh, not guilty, your honor!"

"Not guilty?" the judge yelled. "Why, I saw you with my own eyes. Yer a durn liar, and I'm fining you $5 for fighting and $5 for lying — and no appeal."

And, with a knowing wink at Constable Sullivan, Judge Barney Trainor proved once again he could protect the peace and quiet of East Portland. Sometimes when his court was in a long session, the judge would recess for 10 to 15 minutes, with these instructions:

"Now, no one is to leave the building with this case pending. I realize it's a mite hot in here, so if you want a drink of water, or something else, it's available at the bar in the next room. 'Course, I have to warn you, the water's right out of the river, and somewhat warm. I've been busy, and haven't had time to get to the well for fresh water for awhile. Constable, take charge..."

Judge Trainor is credited with performing one of the fastest marriages on record, when a young couple made a brief stop at his place with the bride's father in hot pursuit. As the irate father rounded a corner, Barney quickly sized up the situation, and told the couple:

"Join hands. In the name of the State of Oregon, I pronounce you man and wife. That'll be $5."

But, the speed with which imbibers were dispatched from one bar to the other probably caused Trainor's "customers" more problems than any. And, naturally, there were complaints. One man swore bitterly when hauled before the judge on a drunkenness charge. He hollered:

"What do you mean I'm drunk, Judge? All I had was a few whiskies!"

Barney Trainor's retort was typical of a saloon-keeping judge:

"You had 15 whiskies, my good man, just as the constable testified. That's enough to make anyone drunk. So, I'm fining you $10 for being drunk in a public place, and another $5 for defamation of my character. Why, you're accusing me of watering down my liquor. NEXT!"

DOC NEWELL

Two leathery mountain men sat before a fire high in the Rockies, the sleet on their beards melting to water as flames jumped from the sputtering logs. Neither spoke for a long period. Then the elder of the two, Robert "Doc" Newell, said:

"Joe, we'd best face it. This life is over. Done. Beaver's all gone from the Rockies. We's going to have to go somewheres else."

His companion, Joe Meek, replied:

"Yup, 'spect you're right, Doc. But, what are we goin' to do? I'm not goin' back to the States."

"No, me neither," Newell said. "Reckon as how I'll go on to the Willamette in Oregon. There's quite a settlement there, and a man can earn his way in that country."

So, in 1840, Joe Meek and Doc Newell, who had become firm friends while tramping the streams and ridges of the Rockies, left the mountains to settle on the Tualatin Plains in Oregon's Willamette Valley. For Robert Newell, it was the second major change in his life. Newell had grown up in Ohio, where he had learned the saddler's trade. But, he had an adventurous disposition, and stories of life in the great West drew him to a trapping party when he was barely out of his teens. A companion once said of Newell:

"There was something different about Doc, even as a kid. He had smarts — not the book-learning kind, but a healthy dose of nature's intelligence. And, he had a force to his character. Made you pay attention to him, even if you disagreed with him. He was a strong man among strong men."

Newell spent the winter of 1832 with the Nez Perce Indians, and it probably was here that he learned some of the ways that earned him the nickname Doctor — or just Doc. An admirer commented:

"Heck, 'ol Doc Newell knew more about fixin' folks than most real doctors. He knowed how to use roots and herbs, and his treatments worked fine for both whites and Indians. Fact is, worked good on horses and dogs, too."

Doc's first wife was a Nez Perce, who went with him to Oregon. She died in 1845, and Doc married Rebecca Newman in 1846. By then Doc had achieved a number of firsts among the settlers in the Willamette Valley. He was the first to bring a wagon to the valley, and was an active participant in the first government organized west of the Rockies. He was a member of the initial legislative committee and the first House of Representatives in Oregon Territory, and even belonged to the first literary and debating club in the territory, the Oregon Lyceum. Doc helped establish the territory's initial newspaper, and was the first man to put keel boats in the Willamette above the falls at Oregon City. And, he did all this in addition to being an outstanding friend and neighbor to his fellow settlers.

Doc's restless ways continued with him, though, and in 1848 he accepted the appointment as Indian commissioner to the Nez Perce, in Walla Walla. A year later he got gold fever and went to California, returning without success to his Oregon home in 1850. There he became the postmaster and general storekeeper, and opened a flour mill at Champoeg in 1855.

Though Doc lost everything except his house in the great Willamette flood of 1861, his service to his neighbors during this trying period won him respect that followed him long beyond his mortal days. As one man remarked:

"Doc was head and shoulders above most of us with his knowledge of government and the way to get things done. But, most of all, he stood tall as a caring neighbor, and a man who was concerned about his fellow beings, regardless of their color or station in life."

Doc returned to the Indian service in 1862, moving his residence to Lewiston, Idaho five years later. Doc died in Lewiston November 14, 1869, closing a chapter on an Oregon pioneer who set high bench marks for others who were to follow him in the new territory.

CAPTAIN MINNIE HILL, RIVER PERSON

Not long after Minnie Mossman married Charles Hill, in 1883, Charlie told his bride:

"Look, Min, you've been talking about coming to work on the boat. Now, were you kidding or were you serious? We're short a man right now and we could use a good hand."

Well, that spurring was all the 20-year-old Minnie Hill needed, and she took her place in the previously all-male world of tug-boating on the Columbia River. Charles Hill was a licensed captain, but because business had been slow, he had left the bridge to work as a deck hand. But, Hill had ambition, and he shared a dream with his wife:

"You're catching on fast, Minnie. And, you know what? I think you should work for your master's license. We could get us a boat then, and you could handle her from the bridge and I'll run the engines."

While they were working on the Cowlitz River, the Hills heard that an old river sloop, the *Jehu*, one of the last river sailing boats, was for sale. They bought the boat, installed engines and a sternwheel, put on a pilot house and cabin, and were ready to go into business for themselves. First, though, Minnie Hill had to take the examination for her master's license, which she passed with ease in 1866. Charlie Hill had great pride in his voice when he told friends:

"Minnie was given a much tougher test for her license than I had for mine. Plain to see those government inspectors didn't want her to pass, but she fooled 'em. She was ready, and did just fine. 'Course she had a good teacher — ME! But, my Min's going to be the first lady river boat captain west of the Mississippi!"

So, at the young age of 23, CAPTAIN Minnie took charge of the Hill's boat, which, not incidentally, had been renamed the *Minnie Hill*. The couple operated the little sternwheeler between Rainier and Cathlamet on the Columbia, with Captain Minnie on the bridge and Captain Charles in charge of the engine. And, begrudgingly, Minnie earned the respect of rivermen. One said:

"Mind you, I don't want this repeated, but Captain Minnie can handle a boat as good as any man. She knows what her engine and her rudder will do, and she can read that river. That's the secret — knowing the water. She's good, that little gal is."

In 1889, the Hills purchased the steamer *Governor Newell*, and once again it was Captain Minnie operating the boat and Captain Charles answering bells in the engine room. And, Captain Minnie soon performed one feat not duplicated by any other Columbia River captain: she gave birth to a son! The lad grew up on the boat until time to go to school.

The *Governor Newell* was retired from service in 1900 and dismantled. At that same time, Captain Minnie decided it was time for her to retire, too, so she moved ashore to become a full-time wife and mother. Captain Minnie was far from dismantled, though, and occasionally would take over on one of the three boats the Hills then owned if another skipper was not available.

Well, Captain Minnie was a modest lady, and she rejected all offers to write articles and books about her life, and turned down the motion picture company that wished to make a feature film about her. She felt there was nothing unusual about her life and her job. So, when Minnie Hill died in Portland in 1946, at the age of 83, she left behind only memories held by oldtimers on the river — memories that have faded with time.

LIGHTING OF MT. HOOD

On July 4, 1887 a small group of mountaineers carrying heavy packs and buffeted by surging winds, struggled up a soft snowfield on Mt. Hood, through drifting clouds. At the base of a rock formation that somewhat resembled a fish's fin, one man called out:

"What you think, Will? Are we high enough? It's going to be hard to go much higher with this load."

The leader of the expedition, Will G. Steel, replied:

"You're right, Frank. I'm sure this is the spot we picked out with the telescope from down below. Besides, it looks even cloudier up above. Let's unload here."

With great relief, the tired men lowered their packs to the snow. Then Will Steel said:

"Let's put all the packs together at the base of the rock. Now, I'm going to stay up here, and anybody else can who wants, though there's no need for everyone to. It won't get dark until after 9:00. I just hope those clouds blow away."

One man remained with Steel, while the others returned to their base camp, several thousand feet below on the mountain. As they left, a climber told Steel:

"You know, Will, now that we're here, I'm not so sure this wasn't a tom fool idea from the very beginning. I don't like the idea of you guys staying up here. Not sure a man can survive a night on the mountain."

"Nonsense," Will replied. "We will be just fine. Besides, we're going to have the biggest bonfire you've ever seen!"

And, that is just what was planned. For what the men had carried to the base of the rock about 2,000 feet below the summit of Mt. Hood was nearly a hundred pounds of lycopodium powder, which, when ignited, would burn a brilliant reddish-orange. By 9:30 p.m., Will Steel and his partner could see the lights of Portland twinkling 50 miles west of their lofty perch. Two hours later, at 11:30 p.m., the dark sky was clear. So, they emptied the powder out of the packs, then touched it off with a torch. Oh, what a blaze! A man in Portland exclaimed:

"Now, there's the way to celebrate the Fourth of July. Have you ever seen fireworks to beat lighting up a mountain?"

The brilliant fire burned for 58 seconds, and was seen clearly in Portland and towns in the Willamette Valley as far south as Corvallis. Reports indicated it was witnessed by nearly 100,000 persons — much of the population of Oregon at the time.

Will Steel and his friends were exhilarated. So much so, in fact, that they immediately vowed to return the next July 4th to ignite an even bigger flare. And, that they did. Their 1888 fire burned for nearly two minutes, and was witnessed by even more thousands than the prior year.

Mt. Hood was illuminated again in 1905, the year of the Lewis and Clark Centennial Exposition in Portland, when Mark Weygandt and five others carried 50 pounds of the red fire powder to the summit of the mountain. Though the flare was smaller than that of Will Steel and his party, it was seen in Portland and Hood River.

Well, the antics of Will Steel and his friends led to the very natural naming of the finny rock that rises to an elevation of 9,500-some feet on the southwestern face of Mt. Hood. The prominent outcropping is called Illumination Rock, in recognition of two glorious Fourths of July and the men who lighted the mountain.

THE CANNON ON THE BEACH

In 1846, the United States war sloop *Shark* was dispatched from the east coast to Oregon Country, both to "show the flag" and to make a survey of the development in the territory at the time. The *Shark* was under the command of Lt. Neil Howison, a young officer with great expectations as to what he would find in the new land.

Captain Howison brought the *Shark* into the Columbia River in July, 1846, and sailed up river to Fort Vancouver, arriving there July 26. Part of the *Shark's* mission was to offset the presence of a British man-of-war at Fort Vancouver. But, what the Americans did not know was that during their long voyage at sea, the United States and Great Britain had signed a treaty that settled most of the border claims between the two countries.

The *Shark* was graciously received at Fort Vancouver, and then at Oregon City, where Oregon's provisional governer, George Abernethy, had a welcoming salute fired by placing black powder in the hole of a blacksmith's anvil. Captain Howison was escorted on a week-long tour of the Willamette Valley, and he later reported:

"I am awed by the natural splendor of this country. . . deep, lush grasses, clear waters, vast forests of native woods. But, I am somewhat disappointed that the settlers have done little in the way of cultivation of the land. . ."

Howison completed his mission in September, 1846, and on September 10, the *Shark* set sail out of the Columbia. But, as the 300-ton sloop was crossing the Columbia River Bar, adverse winds drove the ship onto a sand spit. In order to lighten his vessel, Captain Howison ordered some of her cannons thrown overboard, and her masts shot away. But, the sands held fast, and the ship could not be refloated by her crew. Finally, Howison gave the order to abandon ship.

The three officers and 76 men in the crew of the *Shark* landed safely on Clatsop Spit at the mouth of the Columbia, where they made shelter and built a fire from the wood hull of another sloop that had met the same misfortune at the river's entrance. Then they moved on to nearby Astoria, at that time a settlement of three log buildings and a frame hut. After weeks of negotiation, Captain Howison was able to make arrangements for a ship from the Hudson's Bay Company, and that November sailed with his crew to San Francisco. Before leaving Oregon Country, he sent the Stars and Stripes and the Ensign from the *Shark* to Governor Abernethy, and wrote:

"I cannot omit the occasion to express my gratification and pride that this relic of my late command should be emphatically the first United States flag to wave over the undisputed and purely American territory of Oregon."

The story of the *Shark* could end there, with her flag snapping in the breeze of the newly-claimed territory. But, it does not, for months later, a cannon and capstan from the doomed sloop washed ashore several miles south of the Columba River. For many years these pieces of the vessel could be seen at low water from the small coastal village called Ecola. In 1922, the name of that town was changed officially to Cannon Beach, as the popular resort is known today. And, the *Shark's* cannon was moved to a location on Highway 101, where it was mounted facing the ocean that gave up the trophy by which a town got its unusual name.

CAPTAIN COUCH AND THE MARYLAND

In the course of time, many ships and many captains were important to the establishment of trade routes between the eastern seaboard and the newly-explored territory west of the Mississippi, but perhaps none had greater impact on Oregon commerce than Captain John Couch and the brig *Maryland*.

Captain Couch was just 28 years old when he first arrived at the Columbia River bar in June, 1840. There a seasoned mate told him:

"I've heard she can be a treacherous witch, this Columbia can, Captain. We've got to have the wind just right to go in, or we'll be planting the bowsprit in a sand bar."

Couch watched whitecaps rise at the mouth of the Columbia as sea breezes whipped the water. Finally, with the wind proper for his needs, he ordered full sail, and crossed the bar into the fresh water of the river. He then sailed his ship up the Columbia to the confluence with the Willamette, 120 miles from the ocean, then on up the Willamette to Oregon City, the nerve center of the Oregon Territory. Another captain later remarked:

"You know, Captain Couch made that trip up the Columbia before there were any good charts of the river. He must have had Lady Luck as his pilot and Providence as his steersman — to say nothing of Yankee stubbornness that wouldn't let him turn back."

The *Maryland* was one of the first ocean-going vessels to make the voyage from Astoria to Oregon City. And, after that first trip, Captain Couch sailed in and out of the Columbia and Willamette Rivers several times, proving the possibility of ocean trade to the inland areas of Oregon Territory. But though Captain Couch and the *Maryland* proved that such trade was feasible, that initial voyage from New England was a near-disaster financially. Couch had planned to sell general cargo in Hawaii and in Oregon, then return with salmon and furs from Oregon country, plus whale oil from Hawaii. But, upon his return to Massachusetts, he told his partner, John Cushing:

"John, we were right about the Columbia. It is navigable to the Willamette and above, and there's no question that trade will be established there eventually. But, right now, that fellow McLoughlin of the Hudson's Bay Company has Oregon locked up. I couldn't even buy salmon or furs to take to the Sandwich Islands."

Couch had sold the *Maryland* in the Sandwich Islands (Hawaii), and had returned to New England on a whaler. One thing he took with him from his ship was the portable compass he had used to aid in his navigation around Cape Horn and up the Columbia River. And, though John Couch had had difficulties buying and selling in Oregon country, he was so convinced that sea trade would be profitable that he built another ship, the *Chenamus*, and returned to the Columbia in 1843. This time he began to find a market for goods, and after three trips in and out of the Columbia, decided to open a business in Oregon City. But, upon his return to Massachusetts in 1848, he was again encouraged to go back to sea, this time in command of the *Madonna*, to supply gold-seekers in California. So, Couch brought the *Madonna* to booming San Francisco, where he sold everything aboard at incredible profit, before sailing once again for the Columbia River. This time he opened a warehouse in Portland, and settled down to the life of landlocked merchant, never again taking command of a ship.

But Captain John Couch had proved his point. Commerce between the east coast and Oregon now was common, and he had been a leader in causing it to happen. The New Englander is remembered by a street named for him in Portland, where he lived until his death in 1870. But, perhaps an even more important memento of this sea pioneer is in the Columbia River Maritime Museum at Astoria. It is the portable compass by which he guided his ships at sea and in the rivers. In contrast to today's sophisticated navigation devices it is a crude instrument, yet it served its master well, and helped open the vast Oregon Territory for trade from the sea.

BEAVER MONEY

Money was scarce in the early days of Oregon country, so the pelt of the beaver was a common standard of exchange. But, with the discovery of gold at Sutter's Place in California, gold dust became a plentiful — if somewhat unsatisfactory — trade medium.

When the provisional legislature began arguments whether or not to produce gold coinage for territorial use, one merchant argued before the law-makers:

"Gentlemen, I would be perfectly willing to deal in gold dust if someone would just set a standard value, and also tell me what percentage is gold and what percentage is sand in each bag. But, I'd prefer to see this body begin minting gold coin, and so would my fellow citizens, judging from these petitions I've brought here."

Even though the production of gold coin was clearly in violation of the United States Constitution, the provisional legislature passed an act to engage in the weighing, assaying, melting and stamping of gold. One legislator justified the action by saying:

"We have no choice. The United States has not seen fit to exercise its right to coinage on the Pacific coast, and our citizens are suffering in the exchange."

But, before the Oregon mint could be put into operation, the U.S. Congress established the territorial government in Oregon. Territorial Governor Joseph Lane immediately put a stop to plans for the local government to mint gold. However, Lane's edict did not stop a group of private citizens at Oregon City from forming the Oregon Exchange Company to make $5 and $10 gold pieces. The $5 pieces were 130 grains and the $10 coins 260 grains, all pure gold. Because one side of each coin had a stamped likeness of a beaver, the previous standard of trade, the coins quickly were dubbed "Beaver Money." William Rector, one of the men involved in the minting, later said:

"Money was not particularly elegant up to that time, but I'd say our coins were equally as good as the English coins of George the Third's reign."

Six thousand $5 and 2,850 $10 gold pieces were stamped, with their total value at the time being $58,000. Since the amount of pure gold in the Beaver coins was eight to ten percent more than that in U.S. government gold pieces of similar value, there was no question about redemption of the Beaver money once regular coinage of the United States was put into circulation in Oregon Territory.

Today, a Beaver coin would be worth several thousand dollars, if one could be found. When the San Francisco mint opened in 1854, practically all of the Beaver coins were redeemed at a premium, melted into bullion, and reissued as U.S. coinage. But, Beaver money had served its purpose, assuring citizens of early Oregon a fair exchange until the coin of the realm came to the frontier.

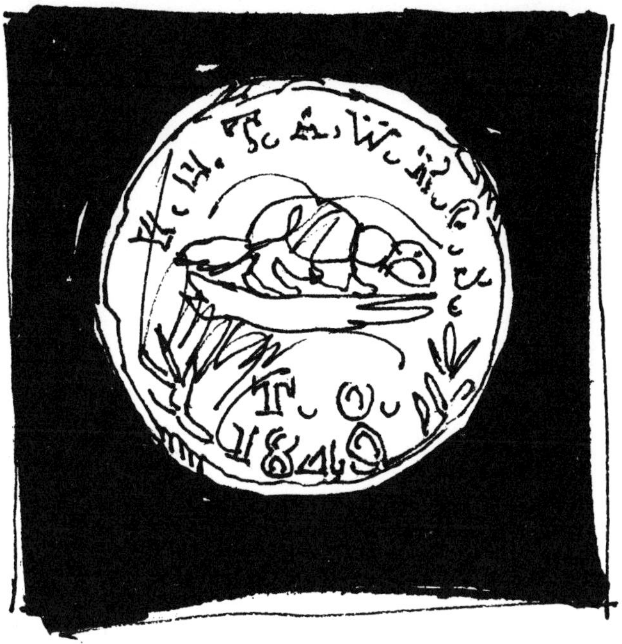
1849

UNCLE JOAB

The huge man in the black, home-spun wool coat, raised a massive fist, and the words exploded from his mouth:

"I am the Al-pha and the O-me-gah' — the beginning and the end. For the righteous, there is no escapin' the love of the Lord, and for the sinners, there's no escapin' His punishing hand. I bring you His words to change the sinners and to keep the foot of the converted from slippin'. . ."

It was Joab Powell, 300 pounds of frontier preacher, extolling his simple beliefs to his faithful followers in Oregon Territory, And Joab Powell — or Uncle Joab as he was called — needed no sanctuary walls to confine his booming voice, or sacramental objects to confirm his faith. Whether on a stump or in a school house, Powell answered his call, and settlers came from miles around to hear the gospel as only he preached it. Not that they *needed* to come too close, for as one man said:

"When Uncle Joab's preachin' outside you can hear him a mile and a half away — two miles if'n the wind is right. We tried him out one day last summer. Say, though, listenin' to Uncle Joab is a right smart treat. Why, he blasts sin and sinners like a wind blowing up a dusty draw. And, let me tell you, if Uncle Joab looks ya' in the eye and asks if'n you've sinned, you'd best fess up. Tryin' to slip a lie past Uncle Joab be 'bout like trying to slide a salmon past a hungry griz . . ."

It is not known for certain whether or not Joab Powell could write his name, but it is known that this remarkable preacher could not read. Born of Baptist parents in Tennessee in 1799, he had no formal education. When he was 19, he married a German girl who spoke a few words of English, but who later developed good command of the language and became Joab's prime teacher. Powell took his growing family to Missouri in 1830, and settled near Independence, the eastern terminus of the Oregon Trail. There he successfully combined farming and preaching. His personal theology was quite simple, keying off the phrase "only good works count." He frequently preached outdoors in Independence, under the shade of a huge walnut tree, which for years after was known as "Joab's Pulpit."

Powell's lack of formal training forced him to rely on his keen retentive memory, in which he developed a rich gospel reservoir. Joab memorized the hymn book he carried, and frequently treated his congregation to renditions in his rich bass. He also was able to quote most chapters of the Bible, thanks to the family readings of Mrs. Powell. From the beginning of their marriage, Joab's wife would read aloud from the Good Book, pausing frequently so that Joab could repeat back the verses he had just heard. As the many children joined the family, the evening ritual continued: Mrs. Powell reading, Joab repeating.

The Powell family came overland to Oregon in 1852, settling on a donation land claim along the Santiam River, where Joab farmed. As time permitted, Powell rode from settlement to settlement in the Willamette Valley on his big sorrel horse, preaching to all who gathered to listen. What his ministry had in soul, it lacked in formality, such as referring to Saint Peter and Saint Paul as General Peter and General Paul. But Powell preached kindness to all men, and he was an ardent abolitionist. Above all, he was earnest and sincere, living the life he intoned.

If Joab Powell had one singular talent, it might have been his understanding of people and knowledge of his audience. That is why, while serving as chaplain of the Oregon legislature, he offered what may have been the most succinct invocation ever given for a body of politicians:

"Lord, forgive them, for they know not what they do!"

ELEPHANT ROCK

For years, one of the most photographed features on the Oregon coast was Elephant Rock, a natural outcropping just south of Otter Crest. The rock resembled a giant elephant, standing in the water with its back to the coastline, its massive trunk resting in the waters of the Pacific.

Siletz Indians, who inhabited this portion of the coast, had an explanation for this inanimate curiosity. Their legend said that many years ago, Fire Demon had raged through the coastal forests, driving animals from their homes to seek refuge in the rivers. Some of the animals followed the streams down to the breakers at the sandy coastline. Finally, Great Spirit met and conquered Fire Demon, but not before miles and miles of the forest had been destroyed. Great Spirit saved some of the fire for sacred use by the Siletz, and protected portions of the forest not yet burned.

It is not told by the Siletz how Great Spirit overcame Fire Demon. Perhaps it was with the help of the lone surviving member of the mammoth jumbo family. When routed from his forest home, he made his way to the ocean. There, he made a final stand, in defiance of the flames behind him. Moving into the water below Otter Crest, he dipped his trunk deep into the sea, and with mighty blows, repeatedly sprayed the cooling water over his back and onto the advancing flames, finally extinguishing the fire.

Great Spirit witnessed the heroic stand of the jumbo, the Indians say, and wished to salute its courage. Deciding that the animal should become a symbol, Great Spirit changed it to stone. Then Great Spirit said that as long as the Siletz followed their tribal customs, Great Spirit and the stone image would watch over the Indians and the lush, green forests where they lived, guarding them from the age-old enemy, Fire Demon.

Elephant Rock remained as pledged by Great Spirit, its head to the setting sun, ever watchful for Fire Demon to break from control. Even the coming of the white man did not change its stance, when the Siletz were forced to maintain themselves on a coastal reservation established in the mid-1850's.

Perhaps what follows is only coincidence. In 1925, the Siletz and Grand Ronde Reservations were dissolved by acts of Congress, drastically changing the lifestyle of the few remaining coastal Indians who had lived in the region near Otter Crest. Shortly thereafter, waves from the Pacific crumbled the head and forequarters of Elephant Rock, leaving only a shapeless hulk. And, it may be just coincidence, too, that not long after the guardian jumbo was destroyed, fire once again raged through the magnificent forest along the coast, in the lands once protected by the Great Spirit.

THE BARMAID WHO CAPTURED FORT GEORGE

There can be little doubt that a lively blond, blue-eyed barmaiden from Portsmouth, England, earned her niche in history because of her physical charms. But, one must, in fairness, admire the courage of Jane Barnes, the first white woman to set foot in Oregon country. For the comely Miss Barnes gave up the relative security of English city life to sail around Cape Horn to the untamed northwest.

Jane Barnes came to Oregon country as the companion of Donald McTavish, governor-to-be of Fort George, the British-owned North West Company fur trading headquarters at the mouth of the Columbia. Prior to leaving Portsmouth on the *Isaac Todd*, Jane enjoyed a shopping spree at McTavish's expense, and the finery she displayed in Oregon made her the center of attention at the trading post after arriving there in April, 1814. That attention increased when Donald McTavish drowned in a boating accident about a month after their arrival, and one man was particularly attentive. He was Cassakas, a son of Comcomly, the latter being the principal chief of the Chinook Indians who inhabited the area. Through an interpreter Cassakas told Miss Barnes:

"If you will become my wife, I will send 100 sea otter skins to your relations. I will never ask you to carry wood, draw water, dig for roots or hunt for provisions. You will be mistress over my four other wives, and can sit at your ease from morning to night. You may wear your own clothes, and you always will have an abundance of fat salmon and elk, and may smoke as many pipes of tobacco during the day as you wish."

Jane was neither flattered nor tempted by Cassakas' offer, and rejected the Chinook summarily. Cassakas, after several attempts to get her to change her mind, left Fort George in a rage, and vowed never to return while Jane was there. Secretly, however, he made plans to kidnap Jane on one of her frequent walks on the beach, a threat that helped confirm plans that McTavish had made prior to his death: passage for Jane back to England.

Jane, meantime, amused herself with violent verbal attacks on the dress and mores of the native Indian women who visited Fort George. She also tried to impress the men at the fort with her intelligence, as well as her good looks. But, on at least one occasion, she was unsuccessful. As told in historical journals, Jane had an argument concerning a phrase from Shakespeare with a well-educated North West Company clerk. The clerk told a friend:

"I"ve just had a conversation with that fine-looking damsel there, who looks down with such contempt on our women, and I'm blessed if she understands a bee from a buffalo."

About five months after arriving at Fort George — which we know now as Astoria —Janes Barnes left Oregon country either on the *Isaac Todd,* as planned, or the schooner *Columbia*. She was next heard from in Canton, China, where, it is reported, she immediately managed to captivate a wealthy English gentleman connected with the East India Company, who offered her a splendid establishment. Alas, misfortune again interrupted Jane's calculations.

By 1816, Jane Barnes had returned to England, and Captain Robson of the *Columbia*, upon which she had sailed from Canton, was attempting to collect money for her passage from the North West Company. Jane claimed she had been promised passage home, and an annuity as well, for the favors she had bestowed on the late Governor McTavish.

The trail of history leaves Jane Barnes at this point, without our knowing whether or not Captain Robson collected his fare, and Jane her annuity. But, Miss Barnes, the first fair-skinned lass to lift her petticoats and walk on Oregon soil, moved out of obscurity and into the folklore of the land with that first step.

THE LOT WHITCOMB

Oregon Territorial Governor John P. Gaines was one of the many dignitaries who travelled to the small village of Milwaukie for the launching of the first steamboat built in the Willamette River on Christmas Day, 1850. Gaines told the ship's builder, Lot Whitcomb, the entrepreneur who had founded Milwaukie:

"She's a beauty, Mr. Whitcomb, a real beauty. You and your men have every reason to be proud of her. She'll be the queen of the rivers."

The 160-foot craft, painted a gleaming white, bore the name of her builder. She was a sound boat, with 140-horsepower engines driving an 18-foot sidewheel. Whitcomb had reasoned:

"With a fine steamer operating out of Milwaukie, we can meet ships in Astoria and bring folks and goods here, instead of having them go to Portland. We'll serve Oregon City, too, since that is where most of the people are."

For master of the *Lot Whitcomb,* the builder had contracted Captain John C. Ainsworth, a capable skipper who had risen to his captaincy on the Mississippi River, then had gone to California during the gold rush. Ainsworth and Whitcomb did not have the best of relationships, for the captain felt he should have been consulted concerning the boat's design and rigging. Captain Ainsworth reputedly said of the man who hired him:

"Whitcomb is ambitious, and with that I have no quarrel. But, he is very vain, and has had little education, and I'm not sure he is entirely trustworthy."

Despite his opinion of the character of his employer, Captain Ainsworth admired the ship, and was surprised it had turned out as well as it had. The *Lot Whitcomb* could steam all day at 12 knots, and could make the run from Astoria to Oregon City in the remarkable time of 10 hours. A regular route was established for the vessel, going between Milwaukie, Oregon City, Portland, Fort Vancouver and Astoria.

But, the fate of the *Lot Whitcomb* was not all glory. Prior to being put into regular service, she went aground on a sand bar at the mouth of the Clackamas River on her maiden voyage to Oregon City. Captain Ainsworth had not yet assumed command, and had, in fact, recommended that the trip be cancelled because of low water. It was two weeks before weirs were built up enough to float the vessel off her sandy perch, much to the chagrin of her namesake. He had insisted on making the trip.

Even though Captain Ainsworth had a reputation for being able to read a ripple better than most seamen could read a chart, he nearly lost the ship New Years Day, 1853. Heavy rains had swollen the Willamette out of its banks, and the current ran wild. Silt and debris rushed by the dock at Oregon City when Ainsworth ordered the *Lot Whitcomb* underway for Milwaukie. But, the current made the ship's rudder nearly useless, and just above Milwaukie, the smart craft was thrown broadside into a submerged rock. As water poured into her hull, Captain Ainsworth headed for the left bank of the river, where the crew barely got a rope around a stout tree before the ship sank. Logs hurtling down the river carried away much of the ship's rigging, and a foot of sand settled in her hull. But, when the river flow receded, the *Lot Whitcomb* was refloated, patched, pumped out, and put back in service nearly a month after the incident.

Thus the *Lot Whitcomb* made history as a pioneer in the dawning territory, helping open the Willamette and the Columbia Rivers to steam travel. But, newer, smaller boats introduced to the river trade were less expensive to operate, and finally the *Lot Whitcomb* was sold to the California Steam Navigation Company. Renamed the *Annie Abernethy,* the proud Oregon vessel finished her days on the Sacramento — still a queen of the rivers.

WHO SAYS IT'S DANDY?

Is there a suburbanite alive today who has not looked out over his expanse of green lawn only to see red as he saw yellow?

Right. Dandelions!

Unfortunately, dandelions are not native to Oregon, and were, in fact, imported by otherwise well-meaning gentlemen. Two have been given credit for bringing the yellow scourge to the northwest, thus earning a special crypt in the gardener's Hades reserved for botanical transporters who upset delicate balances of nature.

A Missourian named Ninevah Ford may well have been the first to bring dandelions to Oregon. It is said that when Ninevah and his wife were preparing to leave Missouri for Oregon in an early 1840's wagon train, Ford told his mate:

"Mother, it's not likely that there's anything growing in Oregon country that will be good for greens. Now, a man has to have greens to go with hog jowls and taters, so I reckon as how we'd better take some seeds and roots to plant there."

How many stories have been written about pioneers crossing the plains who had to throw away plants and fruit trees because of the lack of water or a need to lighten the load? But not the Fords: their dandelion roots and seeds made it to Oregon, where they were duly planted — unleashing this unmitigated pest in virgin territory.

Ninevah Ford got to share the "honor" of bringing the dandelion to Oregon with an early-day Portland physician, Dr. Percy Prettyman. Dr. Prettyman, who received his medical training in Baltimore, was familiar with the medicinal value of herbs, barks and plants. Not long after he settled in Portland, he is reported to have said:

"I have been unable to locate any *Taraxacum officinale* to prescribe for my patients. Its milky juice is valuable as a diuretic and alternative. You know, the botanical name *Taraxacum* is from the Greek, for disquiet or disorder. I guess I shall have to order some seeds from Missouri."

Well, Dr. Prettyman, like Ninevah Ford, did obtain and plant the seeds, and they did well in the rich soils of Oregon. Dr. Prettyman and his sons became well-known in the horticultural affairs of Oregon, exhibiting at fairs and shows, though one wonders if he exhibited the prized *Taraxacum* — better known by its common name, dandelion.

In fairness, though, we must ask: lives there a man or woman who has not thrilled at blowing the down from a dandelion head, or enjoyed fashioning a chain with the plant's stems, or played at checking for "butter" under a friend's chin — or chortled with glee as spots of yellow appeared in a NEIGHBOR'S lawn?

Thanks a lot, Ninevah Ford and Percy Prettyman!

A RIDE OVER THE FALLS

In the fall of 1861, while war ravaged the southern part of this land, a battle of another kind was taking place in Oregon: a conflict with the elements of nature. Sodden clouds had dumped several feet of early snow in the Cascades, and then a warming trend, mixed with heavy rain, began melting the pack. Soon the rivers in northwestern Oregon had risen to flood stage, and by December, many had spilled over their banks.

Houses, barns, and mills floated past Portland as the rampaging Willamette River ripped away the improvements men had made on the land. But, as often is the case, adversity to one is opportunity to another, and for two Portland steamboaters, such was the case. Captain S.R. Smith told his partner, George Taylor:

"I know it's risky, George, but if we're going to get the *St. Clair* down to Portland, now is the time. That water has risen 75 feet below Willamette Falls — why, the falls are darn near flat. Ridin' over sure would be easier than trying to portage around."

So the river boaters plotted a dangerous but exciting trip, one that had never been attempted: taking a small sidewheel steamboat, the *St. Clair*, over Willamette Falls, to get the boat from the upper river to Portland and eventually to the Columbia. The *St. Clair* had been built at Roy's Landing, above Oregon City, two years before. She had been used to haul passengers and freight from Canemah, just above the Willamette Falls, to Harrisburg and Corvallis. But, Taylor and Smith, who had just purchased the boat, wanted the *St. Clair* for the lower Willamette and Columbia River runs, and they had been faced with the difficult task of portaging the boat around the falls. Now, with the high water of early December, they had another choice.

On December 5, 1861, the pair went to Canemah with their engineer, Alonzo Vickers, where they made preparations for the trip. One steamboat already had been destroyed earlier in the week when it broke its moorings and plunged, unmanned, over the cataract. But, the owners were confident they could navigate the falls. They fired the boilers and tested the *St. Clair's* steering, and when they had a head of steam, Captain Smith shouted to well-wishers:

"Cast off those lines. We'll see you below!"

Captain Smith was no stranger to fast-water navigation. He previously had brought the *Shoshone* through the Snake River Canyon, also a first. But, this journey presented a different task: could he keep the flat-bottomed sidewheeler from capsizing as it tipped over the falls?

The *St. Clair* moved slowly away from the Canemah landing, then gained momentum quickly with the force of the water, for the Willamette was flowing at an estimated three times its usual stage. Using a combination of rudder and power, Captain Smith guided the boat through the flood debris in the muddy water. As they approached the falls he shouted to Vickers:

"All right, there's the falls. Doesn't look too bad, but we're going to plunge. Hang on, 'cause here we go!"

Within moments, the little boat bobbed up in an eddy across from the Catholic Church below the falls on the Oregon City side of the river. The boat's tiller rope had broken, but was quickly repaired without serious damage, and the little steamer chugged on toward Portland. A jubilant Captain Smith said:

"Here, let me blow the whistle, to let folks know we're all right."

So, with several blasts on the whistle of the *St. Clair*, S.R. Smith signalled successful navigation of Willamette Falls under steam, a fete that has not been duplicated in the more than 120 years since that historic trip.

THE NIGHT ASTORIA BURNED

A Christmas mood was settling into Astoria early in December, 1922, despite a costly fire in September that had destroyed one of the town's major industries, a lumber mill. But, while most of the town slept in the early morning hours of December 8, a frightening shout echoed through downtown Astoria:

"FIRE! FIRE! SOUND THE ALARM!"

At 2:15 a.m., an alarm was turned in at a fire alarm box at 12th and Commercial, and a pumper truck roared to the downtown site. One of the first men to arrive later said:

"Astoria's downtown section was built on supports, and when I got there, I actually could see four blazes underneath buildings in one block."

Though the source of the fire was to puzzle investigators later on, the thoughts of the firefighters and townspeople in those early minutes were for containment of the blaze. For, unfortunately, Astoria was ready-made for disaster. Many of the buildings in the downtown sector were constructed of wood. But, of even more concern was the fact that these buildings and their streets were built on supports of timbers soaked in creosote, with generous air space between them. At one time the central business district had been built out over the bay, though in 1915, fill had been pumped in at a low level. But, as a firefighter said:

"We always feared just this kind of fire. It wasn't one you could fight head-on, you had to go at it around the edges. But the biggest problem was all that wood. Why, the air space under those streets was just like horizontal chimneys, carrying the flames from one spot another. We'd think we had it stopped at one spot, and it would pop up a block away."

Within an hour after the first alarm, the entire block bounded by Commercial, Bond, 11th and 12th Streets was ablaze, and the fire had spread both east and south of its origin. As the uncontrolled flames raced through the business district, Astorians realized chances of checking the fire downtown were slim. So, merchants tried to empty stock from stores, and valuable possessions were moved out. Many citizens saw their lifetime efforts explode in flames as the fire jumped relentlessly from building to building, block to block. Finally, hope was expressed:

"They're holding the fire in check on the north side, but that's about the only place. They've got water over there. It's getting close to the hospital on the east side, and the only way we're going to stop it is to blast some buildings to make a fire break."

A truck was sent to a nearby logging camp for dynamite, and loggers familiar with the use of the explosive were drafted to do the blasting in the fire area. In the end, this drastic move checked the fire on three sides, but not until nearly 30 blocks in the business section of Astoria had been devastated by the flames. Damages totaled in the millions of dollars, for more than 220 stores, shops, rooming houses and other commercial establishments were destroyed. Some 2,000 persons lost their homes. Three persons died while the fire was in progress, though none from burns.

In nine hours, Oregon's oldest city was reduced to a charred mass, fringed by a few business houses and homes located on the high ground, away from the destruction. But Astoria's spirit was not seared, and the town began rebuilding immediately. Some businesses even were back in operation by Christmas.

Today, Astoria bears few of the scars of this disaster six decades ago, for streets were filled and widened, and new buildings of stone and concrete replaced their wooden ancestors that fell to the fire demon. And, though most modern Astorians had no personal experience with the fire, now and then the haunting questions of "who" and "how" and "why" stir memories in this modest city by the sea.

THE STAR OF OREGON

Settlers arriving in the Willamette Valley in the early 1840's found themselves in the land of plenty, but with one important exception: livestock. It was the rare individual who, at that time, got to Oregon with any animals, and most of the livestock in the valley was owned by the Hudson's Bay Company. The avowed policy of the Hudson's Bay Company was to discourage private ownership of cattle, sheep and horses. Animals could be leased from the company, but purchase prices were so high it was virtually impossible to buy stock.

Finally, a group of men met to seek ways to bring in stock. One man made a suggestion:

"Look, why don't we build a ship and sail it to San Francisco. We can either earn money with it there to buy stock, or trade it for animals. Let's talk to Felix Hathaway and Joe Gale. Hathaway was a shipbuilder in Boston 'fore he came out, and ol' Joe once was a seaman."

The group decided to form a company to build a vessel. Felix Hathaway agreed to help design the ship — the first to be built in Oregon — and to serve as her captain. But, for mountain man Joe Gale, it was another matter. Gale told the group:

"You've got a good idea, all right, but I've given my word to help set up that settlement out on the Tualatin Plains. Tell you what. When you're far enough along so's you're sure you'll get 'er built, I'll throw in with you."

So, the craftsmen began their task on an island in the Willamette River, below what was to become Portland. By May of 1841, the *Star of Oregon* was ready to be launched. Hathaway had left the project, but Joe Gale took charge. One major problem remained, that of getting sailcloth for the ship. The only source in the region was the Hudson's Bay Company headquarters at Fort Vancouver, where a skeptical Dr. John McLoughlin said:

"Huh, you men are just building a coffin for yourselves. I know Joe Gale. He's been a hunter and a trapper for years, but what does he, or for that matter, any of the rest of you, know about navigating a ship at sea?"

Through the intervention of Commodore Charles Wilkes, U.S. Navy, Dr. McLoughlin relented, and sailcloth, paint, and handling lines were traded for wheat and furs. It was September, 1842, when the 56-foot *Star of Oregon*, with Joe Gale in command, at last sailed down the Willamette and Columbia Rivers to the Pacific — where most of her makeshift crew immediately became seasick! Gale, alone, managed to keep the ship heading south, standing one 36-hour watch on the helm himself.

But, despite heavy seas and thick clouds that masked the shoreline, Gale's navigation was accurate, and on September 17, the *Star* broke through fog at the entrance to San Francisco harbor. Her crew rejoiced in raucous celebration.

The *Star of Oregon* was traded to Jose I. Lamonture for 350 head of cattle, to be delivered the following spring, since Gale felt it was too late to begin a drive to Oregon that fall. The enterprising skipper then circulated fliers extolling the virtues of Oregon, suggesting that others bring stock and join the cattle drive north in 1843.

By mid-May, 1843, Gale was able to muster a company of 42 men, and when they headed north they drove some 1,250 cattle, 600 horses and mules, and about 3,000 sheep. They arrived in the Willamette Valley 10 weeks later, where the animals were distributed to eager homesteaders. Thus the livestock monopoly was broken, and a great industry started — all through the will of a few men and the first vessel built in Oregon's waters.

DISASTER AT CANEMAH

In the 1850's, one of the centers of shipbuilding on the Willamette River was at Canemah, the major river port just above Willamette Falls and the territorial capitol of Oregon City.

Ten river boats were built at Canemah that decade, including the *Gazelle*, a 145-foot sidewheeler that was the second boat to be launched there. Canemah boats worked the stretches of the upper river, linking Oregon City to Salem, Eugene, Corvallis, and other river towns. So, when the *Gazelle* splashed into the river in March, 1854, she set out on a trial run of 80 miles to Corvallis. But, the steamer only got as far as Salem, half her expected run, where Captain Robert Hereford gave assistance to another river boat, the *Oregon*. The *Oregon* had hit a snag in the river, and was sunk in about 8 feet of water. Hereford took the *Gazelle* alongside, so that cargo from the *Oregon* could be unloaded. But, as the *Oregon* was lightened, she capsized, and only quick action getting away from her saved the *Gazelle*.

Captain Hereford returned the *Gazelle* to Canemah with cargo from the *Oregon*, and reported a few minor problems he had discovered on the maiden voyage. These were corrected, and on April 8, 1854, *Gazelle* was ready for her first regular trip up river to Corvallis. About an hour after daybreak, passengers were loaded at Linn City, across the Willamette from Canemah, and then the boat steamed across the river to the Canemah dock and began loading passengers and freight. As heavy smoke poured from the stack of the *Gazelle*, one of her deck hands said to a shipmate:

"Say, isn't that the engineer leaving the boat? Sure looks like he's in a hurry to get somewhere. Why would he be leaving now?"

But that sailor's question was never answered, for just then the boiler of the *Gazelle* exploded with a shattering BOOM, hurling cargo and debris over a wide area. Of the 60 persons on board the ship, 24 were killed, and another 30 injured. Stores and workshops in Canemah and Oregon City were closed for the day as workers and residents hurried to the disaster scene to help rescue and treat survivors.

A coronor's jury was seated to investigate the accident. One survivor who testified was Captain Hereford, but he could provide little help as to the cause of the explosion. Hereford was found innocent of any negligence.

One who was *not* considered innocent was the ship's engineer, Moses Tonie, who could not be located. The jury declared Tonie guilty of gross and culpable negligence. But, that finding did not answer the questions that were in the minds and on the lips of citizens at Canemah for years to come. As one man put it:

"Some say the *Gazelle* had a faulty boiler, or a defective water pump. I say find Moses Tonie and you'll find out what happened to that boat. Maybe it's just a rumor, and maybe it's true that Tonie tied down the safety valve on that boiler so's she'd blow. Some say he was paid to do it. Only one way to find out — find Moses Tonie."

Only the hull of the *Gazelle* was salvaged, and that was floated over Willamette Falls under the control of shore lines, and rebuilt as the steamer *Senorita* to operate on the lower Willamette and Columbia Rivers. But Moses Tonie, the engineer who held to answer to the disaster at Canemah, never was heard from again.

A BUGGING OF VERNONIA

Wire taps and other electronic listening devices have become somewhat commonplace in today's society, but little of the sophisticated modern equipment could "bug" a whole town, as once happened in Vernonia, Oregon.

It came about quite by accident, and was all very innocent — with no sinister spy ring, criminal element, or even a law enforcement agency involved. But, it did provide hours of enjoyment and a private joke for a one-time prominent citizen of Vernonia: E.E. Hayes.

Mr. Hayes moved to Vernonia in the early 1920's, to build and manage a mill for the Oregon-American Lumber Company. One of the first things he bought, after completing houses for his family and for the mill workers, was a radio — a beautiful Atwater-Kent "bread board" model. Mr. Hayes once recalled:

"I'd get home from the mill about 5:30 or so, and I liked to turn on the radio and see what stations I could pick up. I could get Portland, and sometimes a station down in Beaumont, Texas, only 30 miles from where I was born. Oh, I was fascinated with that radio! One night I was fiddlin' around with the set, and not getting much. Then I picked up what I thought was a station, only I heard a telephone ring. Pretty quick Central — the operator — answered. Well, by golly it was someone in Portland calling Vernonia, and I heard the whole conversation."

E.E. Hayes wasn't about to tell anyone in Vernonia that he had the town bugged, for this was better than real radio anyday. He recalled one conversation he heard very well:

"Two women were talking, and one of them said, 'Say, did you hear the news at Oregon-American today? Ol' Man Hayes fired So-and-So, 'cause he caught him boot-legging liquor into the mill!' Well, heck, I was Old Man Hayes, and I was only about 40 at the time."

It may have been the same two women Hayes listened to another time when they were talking about rhubarb pie:

"I'd never heard of rhubarb pie until I came to Oregon, and I'd had some that was good and some that was bad. This sounded pretty good. So, when one woman asked the other for her recipe, I copied it down, too. Thanks to those two ladies, I've been enjoying rhubarb pie for more than 50 years."

Mr. Hayes learned that his radio was a "regenerative" set, and was picking up telephone conversations from the ground wire of the telephone line that was near his front porch. His bugging of the hamlet of Vernonia stopped in 1926 when he moved to Longview, Washington. And, even though he wrote a newspaper column in Longview, and kept active with the public, he never revealed all he knew about the people of Vernonia, or how he came to learn it, to anyone except his family. In fact there may still be some old timers in Vernonia who to this day don't know they once were bugged.

Well, at least they *didn't* know.

THE HAYBURNER

Steamships had been running the Willamette River between Oregon City and Eugene for more than a decade when an erstwhile inventor in Corvallis decided he could cash in on the competition for passengers and cargo in 1860. He told a neighbor:

"Yup, believe I've got the answer to the high costs of steamships. The one thing we've got more of than anything else in this here valley is grass. And while you can't burn grass in a boiler, you can burn hay in a cow, so t' speak. So I'm riggin' up a boat with a treadmill. I'll put cattle on it, and when they walk on the treadmill to get the hay, it'll drive the wheel. Oh, it's a sure winner — 'n a durn sight cheaper than those steamers they got puffin' and blowin' up 'n down the river."

Well, this inventive genius — who has remained nameless in the 120 years since he launched his boat — did just as he said he would. His craft was a small scow, shallow of draft, but capable of hauling a fairly good payload. Or so he thought. Once in the water, the scow performed well for several miles, until his power source decided it was time to take a rest. Then the skipper lost control and the boat went aground at McGoolin's Slough, below Corvallis. When stopped, the cattle somehow managed to get to the rest of the hay, and they devoured the boat's fuel.

Fortunately, the steamer *Onward* came along, and tugged the scow back into the river. Once in the current of the Willamette, the little boat proceeded on down stream to Canemah, the main landing above Willamette Falls and Oregon City. There the little vessel was a curiosity for all. A grizzled river man took one look and snorted:

"Bah! Cattle power! On a boat? Why, I wouldn't hook those mangy hayburners to a wagon, least alone try to drive a boat with 'em. That man must be tetched!"

Undaunted, the skipper took on another load of hay and started back up river. That was when he learned the hard way that cattle power was not necessarily the same horsepower as water power, for he could barely make headway against the current. Luckily, he was able to get his craft back to the Canemah landing, and thus was not swept over Willamette Falls.

Once ashore, the inventor sold the boat and the cattle, and abandoned the project. When last heard from, he was slinking away, muttering:

"Well, it may have been a failure, but I refuse to be cowed by the experience."

73

THE PETER IREDALE

About 8:00 a.m. on a blustery October day in 1906, Bob Farley, first mate of the Point Adams Coast Guard Life Saving Station, was walking along the beach with his small dog.

Suddenly, the dog began barking, and running up and down a small sand dune. Farley climbed to the top of the dune, where he barely could look out to sea through the rain squalls and blowing foam. But, he said:

"You're right, boy! You're right! There IS something out there. Yup . . . a ship, and she's aground in the breakers!"

Farley ran to nearby Fort Stevens, where he alerted the life saving team at the Coast Guard Station, thus giving first notice to the world of the marine disaster that was to become Oregon's most famous shipwreck: the *Peter Iredale*.

Farley continued to act. Ripping the red lining from a soldier's coat at Fort Stevens, he dashed back to the beach. Then, after tying the lining on a long pole, he waded out in the surf as far as he could go, waving the pole from side to side to tell the men on the vessel that help was on the way. A young seaman named McIlroy was about to try to swim to shore when another sailor shouted:

"Captain. Look, there on the beach. A bloke's signaling to us. Help's coming."

Perhaps the *Peter Iredale's* fate had been determined in the early hours of the morning, when she arrived off the mouth of the Columbia in high winds and a churning sea. Her master, Captain Lawrence, decided to hold the big sailing vessel off shore until first light, when a pilot could help take her across the Columbia River Bar. He ordered her sails shortened while waiting.

But the wind and the sea can play cruel tricks on mere men, and shortly before dawn, without warning, the *Peter Iredale* was blown onto Clatsop Spit, a final resting place for many another proud vessel. She soon was fast aground.

Quick action by Bob Farley and the Coast Guard crew saved the lives of all the British sailors aboard the *Peter Iredale,* who were removed from the ship without injury. And, though she was solidly aground, the *Peter Iredale's* hull was not damaged. Her captain and owners were confident that she could be towed stern first through the breakers into deep water, where once again she would cut through the world's seas.

Not so, as any visitor to the north Oregon coast in the last three-quarters of a century knows. As days and weeks passed, the *Peter Iredale* assumed a starboard list in the clinching sand, which never released its grip on the 278-foot ship. Finally, salvage attempts were abandoned.

Little remains of the iron-ribbed *Peter Iredale* save her skeletal hull, still fast aground at Fort Stevens State Park, a haunting reminder to sailors and land-lubbers alike of the eternal power of the sands and the sea.

THE RIVER THAT DRAINED THE WEST

Weird topographical concepts and long-lived myths emerged in the early days of this land concerning the unusual geography of the Great Basin of the West. Not the least of these was a myth concerning a single river believed to run from the Rocky Mountains to the Pacific.

Some of the stories that supported the myth originated with the Indians in the coastal and mountain areas, but the legend received credence from the Spanish, English and American explorers who penetrated the region beyond the Rockies in the late 18th and early 19th centuries.

Not the least of those explorers who gave substance to the myth were William Clark and Meriwether Lewis. The leaders of the famous expedition had missed the mouth of the river now known as the Willamette both on their voyage down the Columbia and on their return trip. But, on the return, they learned that a large valley lying south of the Columbia — which they had assumed was drained by the Quicksand River — held another, even larger river, that fed into the Columbia. The Indians called it the Multnomah. Captain Clark said:

"If what the Indians tell us is true, there is a river of considerable size that flows into the south side of the Columbia below where we are camped now. I feel I must go back to verify this information."

So, Clark took a small group of men back down the Columbia, and the next day entered the mouth of the Willamette, which had been screened from view during their earlier passage by islands in the Columbia. He named the river Multnomah, the designation applied by local Indians only to the channel between the islands and its outlet. Clark was told of falls on the river some distance from its mouth, but apparently did not travel that far up the Willamette, or Multnomah, as he called it. He later wrote:

"I am satisfied of the size and magnitude of this great river which must water the vast tract of country between the western range of mountains and those of the sea coast as far south as the waters of California. . ."

An Indian in the area sketched a map for William Clark, in which distances were greatly overestimated. This drawing was later used for the first map of the region, establishing astounding geographic misconceptions that were repeated by many cartographers for years to come.

But, William Clark was not the only one to exaggerate the length of the "Multnomah." Trappers, explorers and mountain men frequently overestimated the distances involved in the Willamette Valley, causing map makers to believe that the Multnomah had its source in the Rocky Mountains. Even one of the most noted cartographers of his day, John Melish, of Philadelphia, extended the Multnomah clear to the Great Salt Lake, in Utah. Reference to the Multnomah on the Melish map was considered in treaty negotations in 1819, when the southern boundary of Oregon Territory was being settled with Spain. Luckily, references to the Multnomah were omitted from the final settlement.

This vast, unplatted region of the west continued to give explorers problems well into the 19th century, even as more and more people came to Oregon country. As late as 1825, some thought the Multnomah to be several hundred miles long, and to drain the Rockies. Finally, in 1834, Hudson's Bay Company cartographer John Arrowsmith, working from the notes of British explorer Peter Ogden, published the first maps that abolished the mythical creations of previous charts. Only then did the trappers, explorers and settlers of the beautiful Willamette Valley learn that the mouth of their river — the mythical Multnomah — was, indeed, only 150 miles from its rise in Oregon's Cascade Mountains.

CAPTAIN WAKEMAN AND THE NEW WORLD

Shortly before the steamship *New World* was to depart from New York for the West Coast, the sheriff of New York boarded the ship, accompanied by three deputies. The lawman told Captain Edgar Wakeman:

"Captain, your departure is going to be delayed indefinitely. Papers have been served on the owners of this ship and I am seizing it for debt payment."

Captain Wakeman stroked his chin, then said:

"Hmmm, I see, Sheriff. But, if we're going to be here long, I would like to work my engines, to keep rust from accumulating in the boilers."

The sheriff agreed, and Captain Wakeman told his chief engineer to build up a full head of steam. When the ship was ready, Wakeman ordered deckhands to chop the retaining hausers with an axe, and moments later the *New World* was heading out of New York Harbor. When the sheriff realized Captain Wakeman's intentions, he drew a pistol, saying:

"Captain, I must remind you that this vessel is in my charge. Now return to the dock."

"On the contrary, Sir. I am master of this ship, and she now is afloat on the high seas. She is in my charge, and anyone who questions my authority will meet dire consequences."

With that retort, Captain Wakeman ordered all hands on deck, where they appeared armed with pistols and knives. The sheriff knew he had chosen the wrong time to challenge the captain, and raised no objections when he and his deputies were put in a small boat to be rowed ashore.

With his "guests" dispatched, Captain Wakeman set course for South America and the trip around the Horn. But, since the vessel was steaming without proper authorization papers, it was necessary to enter harbors at night, and to escape from authorities who had been ordered to detain the ship. En route to Rio de Janeiro, the *New World* had to outrun a British frigate seeking to overhaul it, for without papers, the ship was a legal prize if taken in international waters. In Rio, Captain Wakeman feigned an accident while getting into a small boat, and told the American consul:

"Sir, I slipped and fell into the water when coming ashore to pay my respects. I dropped my dispatch case and I'm afraid I've lost my sailing papers."

The consul drew up new papers, but before they were ready, yellow fever swept the *New World* forcing its quarantine. Eighteen of her crew died. Captain Wakeman had her coal bunkers loaded, and once again ignoring authority, slipped out of the harbor at night. The *New World* rounded Cape Horn without incident, but news of her flight had preceded her, and when she went into Valparaiso for provisions, the ship was seized once again and ordered into quarantine for 20 days. Threat of severe reprisal kept Captain Wakeman under control for eight days, but then he once more exercised his own brand of daring, and slipped his ship out of the harbor under the dark of night. Wakeman dodged authorities all the way up the west coast of the Americas, and even boldly entered Panama to pick up gold seekers wanting passage to California when he learned there was not enough militia in the city to hold his ship.

Well, the defiant Captain Wakeman delivered the *New World* to its owners in San Francisco on July 30, 1850, and thereafter she was used for passenger service between San Francisco and Sacramento for several years. In April, 1865, the *New World* was purchased by the Oregon Steam Navigation Company, and was brought to Portland for service on the Portland-Cascade route in the Columbia River. In Oregon she continued to attract attention, one time bringing out more than a ton of gold from the mines of eastern Oregon and Idaho, and on another occasion setting a record of 6 hours, 57 minutes for the round trip on the Portland-Cascades run.

But, no voyage of the *New World* was as eventful as her first, and no skipper as audacious as Edgar Wakeman, the captain for whom the law of the sea outweighed the law of the land, time and again.